THE
SIGNS

THE
SIGNS

The new science of how to trust your instincts

DR TARA SWART

flightbooks

Flight Books, part of Flight Studio, a Flight Group company

In collaboration with Ebury Publishing

UK | USA | Canada | Ireland | Australia
India | New Zealand | South Africa

Ebury Publishing is part of the Penguin Random House group of companies
whose addresses can be found at global.penguinrandomhouse.com

Penguin Random House UK
One Embassy Gardens, 8 Viaduct Gardens, London SW11 7BW

penguin.co.uk
global.penguinrandomhouse.com

First published by Ebury Publishing/Flight Books in 2025
2

Copyright © Tara Swart 2025
Illustrations © Joséphine Grenier
Cowriter: Paul Murphy
The moral right of the author has been asserted.

Typeset in 10.5/14.5pt Sabon LT Std by Six Red Marbles UK, Thetford, Norfolk
Printed and bound in India by Thomson Press India Private Limited

The authorised representative in the EEA is Penguin Random House Ireland,
Morrison Chambers, 32 Nassau Street, Dublin D02 YH68

A CIP catalogue record for this book is available from the British Library

Hardback ISBN 9781846048494
Trade paperback ISBN 9781846048500

Penguin Random House is committed to a sustainable future
for our business, our readers and our planet. This book is made
from Forest Stewardship Council® certified paper.

For Robin Bieber, the love of all my lifetimes.

Contents

PREFACE

HOW I CAME TO SEE LIFE IN TECHNICOLOUR

n the first few weeks after I lost my beautiful husband Robin to leukaemia, the strangest thing happened: I kept seeing robins in the garden. I had heard various stories in which people said that lost loved ones sometimes appeared soon after their deaths in the form of various birds, and there is even a saying, 'robins appear when loved ones are near', but I still thought it was strange. I'd never seen robins in the garden so often, yet, for a few weeks, every time I went to the French windows, a robin appeared. Then, one day, they stopped, and I never saw them so frequently again.

Despite growing up in a household in which spirituality was a daily presence, my parents always emphasised the importance of education, and science in particular. I was encouraged to become a doctor, which I did after studying preclinical medicine for two years, a BSc for one year, a PhD in neuroscience for three years and then clinical medicine for three years. I did the required year of medical and surgical jobs, then worked as a doctor specialising in psychiatry for six years before transitioning to become an executive adviser and a professor at the business school at Massachusetts Institute of Technology (MIT). My professional world was one of science and logic, and everything I had been taught primed me to doubt that the robins in my garden could be anything but coincidence. A small part of my mind wanted to believe that seeing them meant something, but the rational part could not. Over time, I have learnt to give that small part more respect. This book is informed by the journey I took: from dismissing the things I couldn't explain to accepting and even embracing them, allowing the signs I notice to show me a way forward.

I felt terribly lost and was desperately searching for answers when Robin died. It was four excruciating months from diagnosis to death. Despite my resilience, and knowledge of neuroscience and psychology, I was not equipped to deal with the level of devastation when he actually passed away. I had believed that, with me, his loving wife and a medic, by his side, he would make it. This belief was based on his unconditional love for me, and my ability to utilise the powers of visualisation and manifestation, skills that I had spent years developing with much success, and which I wrote about in my previous book, *The Source.** I never allowed any level of doubt to creep into this unwavering belief. But he didn't make it. He could not. The leukaemia was too ravaging, and the treatment itself was brutal. I was left falling into a bottomless pit of grief and despair, and I didn't know how I was going to make it out. I was a widow in my forties with a future ahead of me that would be nothing like what I had imagined. I found myself struggling, with no idea of how I would cope day to day, let alone heal over time, without him there and with my world view about love and abundance shattered.

Despite my scepticism, I kept thinking about the robins. Then, about six weeks after Robin died, I was woken by an almighty thump on my shoulder at around 4am. As my eyes

---

* In that book, I wrote about my conception of manifestation, as informed by my background as a neuroscientist, describing how you can visualise positive outcomes to keep your brain in a state of hope and abundance, and thereby create the real-world actions that are more likely to favour the outcomes you desire.

acclimatised to the darkness, I saw Robin standing right next to my bed. He was becoming more and more solid, as though he was pushing himself through treacle to make himself seen. I was shocked and transfixed, and could sense the level of effort he was making. As soon as he became so fully formed that I could see the outline of his hair and face, he started to dissolve from the top down, and the last thing I saw were his shins and feet before he was gone, and I gasped out loud.

As soon as I woke up again the next morning, I googled 'Is it possible to see a deceased loved one?' and the answer I found was that up to 60 per cent of older people in grief experience 'visual hallucinations'. I remember thinking how sad it was that something that felt so profound was dismissed as being a hallucination rather than discussing whether it was actually possible or not. I knew that I was fully awake and not dreaming, and despite what my years of medical training and scientific thinking had taught me to believe, I was very sure of what I had seen.

I started speaking to more people about what had happened and heard many similar stories in return. And when I googled the same thing again during the writing of this book, three years later, the answer I got was different: 'Yes, it's normal to see, hear or sense a deceased loved one ... [and these experiences] are usually comforting and benign.' Some people attribute these experiences to the brain expecting to see someone we are close to and filling in the gaps in response to relevant external cues.[1] But I was certainly not expecting to see Robin at that time, as I had been fast asleep immediately before being jolted wide awake, and in my waking hours I was painfully aware of the fact that he was gone. One opinion piece I read on the back of this search speculated that gene variants or brain chemistry might allow people to perceive the deceased.[2] Dr David Hamilton speculated that ancient people who could perceive the deceased, and therefore believed in an afterlife, would be less likely to fear death. As a result, they would take more risks that would potentially mean that the genes that allow this type of spirit vision would eventually be lost from the human race. However, there would still be some ancient gene variants in the human race today, so there might be some people around now who are capable of seeing the spirits of dead people in the form that would be most recognisable to them. Although there is no scientific proof of this, as a brain scientist, the idea got me intrigued about the nature of consciousness and what we are actually capable of. It also made me question whether only things that can be proven scientifically are important as part of the human experience.

A few days after seeing Robin by my bed, I told my friend Alice about what had happened. A few weeks later when I received her Christmas card, she had written, 'I'm so glad you saw Robin. I knew you would.' In the new year, I was having dinner with her, and I asked her how she knew I was going to see him. Matter-of-factly, she replied, 'He came to me in a dream and told me he was going to visit you.'

As my world fell apart and I attempted to navigate my way through my deepest loss, I came to the understanding that mainstream science can't answer every question, and conversations like the one with Alice got me questioning not only what we can perceive but also whether we can remain connected to the spirits of those we have lost.

I began to realise that the solutions didn't all reside within me. I had previously believed that I had the power to create the life I wanted, but the action boards,* visualisation, affirmation and manifestation techniques I had spent years perfecting had lost their lustre. It was clear that they were not going to appease my grief, and as such it was an extremely disheartening time. I needed to find something to guide me on a new path. Regardless

---

* These are like vision boards, but I believe you need to take action to make things happen, hence why I came up with the new name for them. Again, this is something that I discussed in more detail in *The Source*.

of my background as a neuroscientist and psychiatrist, as well as a hugely supportive community – resources that I know not everyone has – I could no longer count on those skills that had served me so well in the past.

In particular, I felt as though I had lost access to the intuition that I had come to rely on so much that I called it my super-power. By this I mean that I had always had a strong sense of knowing the right way forward for me, and I had used years of journalling and reading back over entries to trust my instinctive decision-making and make it work for me. But I did not feel that I could trust myself in the state I was in, and I had no idea how to move forward. However, despite my devastation, I had a tiny glimmer of hope that I could adapt, find a new direction and reconnect to my intuition; in fact, I knew I had no other choice.

Out of desperation, a few months after Robin died, I decided to consult a medium, and I saw another one about six months later. Some of what they shared resonated with me, but I was sceptical. I felt that much of what they said to me could have been researched on the internet or social media, and a lot of it did not make sense at the time or later. Fuelled by my sense of self-reliance, along with a belief in my ability to optimise my brain, I remember thinking, 'If it is possible to open channels of communication with those who have passed, and Robin was my husband, best friend and twin flame, then I should be able to do it myself.'

I had begun to get a glimpse of this kind of unexplained com-munication when Robin's life was coming to an end. The day he died, he called to me before I had risen for the day, to help him sip some water because he could no longer raise a glass to his lips. I was exhausted, and he looked at me with concern and told me he loved me. As I returned to the sofa around the corner, where I slept each night to remain close to him if he needed me, and started to fall back to sleep, I saw a still image of his face in my mind looking healthy – he looked like he did in a picture I'd taken of him on holiday a few years before. He then said to me one word: 'celebrate'. I couldn't make sense of it at the time, but I later took this to mean that I must celebrate the fact that I was still alive and live in a purposeful way, even though I had to do so without him. This spiritual experience of a person coming to say goodbye before they die is something that I have since heard other people describe. Robin passed away at lunchtime that day when I had just gone into the kitchen, where his hospital bed was, to get some soup and sit with him.

With these experiences in mind, I began to use my training as a neuroscientist to question how the brain is affected by grief and explore spiritual practices that address death but lie beyond the boundaries of known science. For example, I researched near-death experiences and terminal lucidity as ways to understand if consciousness can exist apart from the physical body (we'll explore these in more detail in Chapter 1). When Robin passed away, I had an overwhelming sense of knowing that the body lying in the bed was not him and that the essence of who he was lay beyond this vessel. This, over time, allowed me to reframe my relationship with my own and others' mortality in a way that gave me reassurance and a renewed sense of optimism for the future. It also made me increasingly certain that there's more to consciousness than we can explain, and I want to share the evidence for this with you in this book.

As I opened my mind to what could be possible, more signs slowly but surely began to present themselves to me. I started to notice hearts all around, and then I began to see what I thought might be signs from Robin, such as certain songs of significance to us, more sightings of robins, either seen with or reported by other people, and people passing on messages to me that they had received from Robin in their dreams. At first, these appeared randomly and were few and far between, but eventually they appeared more often and were clearer. And not all of the signs I was receiving were from Robin. For example, in

December 2023, I wrote in my journal that because my father, who passed away three months after Robin, had once responded 'over my dead body' when I'd told him that my English teacher at school had suggested I could become an actress, if I now had his permission from the other side, I would bump into a famous actress. A couple of weeks later, I attended the Christmas carol service for the Lady Garden Foundation, a charity that I am a trustee of. I was standing near the entrance with my friend when a woman approached us. I tried to step out of her way, but we both moved in the same direction, and we literally bumped into one another. She said sorry and then walked on. I said to my friend, 'Oh my goodness, that was Anna Friel – I love her.' It was only when I next read back through my journal that I saw the entry about my father. It still shocks me every time a new thing like this happens. I sent Anna a message to thank her for doing a reading for our charity, and she responded a few days later to say that her brother, who is a doctor, had sent her a podcast to watch on YouTube and the episode of *The Diary of a CEO* that I appeared on popped up after it, so she'd watched it and had been telling all her friends and family about me before she had seen my message.

As things progressed, I got an inkling that Robin might be communicating with me through numbers, which made sense, as he had worked in finance and been obsessed with the Fibonacci series,* for example. So, I thought I would test out my theory by asking him in my mind to send me certain numbers on significant dates such as anniversaries. The first time I was really sure Robin had sent me a number sign was around the first anniversary of his passing. In the week beforehand, I'd started

---

* The Fibonacci series is a sequence of numbers in which each number is the sum of the two numbers before it: 0, 1, 1, 2, 3, 5, 8, 13, etc. The sequence can often be seen in nature; for example, in the family trees of honeybees and the spiral arrangement of pine cones and shells.

to see the numbers 1, 11 and 100 everywhere I looked – for example, on my phone, registration plates, clocks and social media – and on the actual day of the anniversary, I received a significant message via the number 108, which is a very spiritual number. In Hinduism, it represents the wholeness of existence and divine connection, and it has associations to sacred texts and practices like mantra chanting, with verses repeated 108 times, and prayer bead necklaces, which have 108 beads. Things like this continued to happen in the most astonishing ways and became more timely and exact, such that on the second anniversary I asked for and received a sign of 200 just after midnight on Instagram that lasted for the whole day of the anniversary and had changed to 201 by the next day.

Also, on the day of the second anniversary of his passing, I was due to leave the Navajo Nation, where I'd been filming for a week, and fly direct to LA, but I found out at the last minute that I was going to have to make a transfer. I'd previously asked Robin to send me a sign of a phoenix on that trip, because I was beginning to feel like I was re-emerging as someone new after having burnt myself out, and it was unusual enough to not be put down to coincidence. Before going to the Navajo Nation, I'd spent a week in Oklahoma City, where the studio was. While there, I kept passing a Chinese restaurant called the Phoenix Garden on the way from my hotel, and, when my flight was booked from Flagstaff, Arizona, the transfer was through Phoenix. Some time later, back in London, a road was blocked off as I was walking home one day, so I had to take a diversion down a small and pretty side street. I remember feeling sure that I would get a sign – it was just a strong sense of knowing (sometimes people refer to this as claircognisance) – and, when I turned the corner, I came across a pub with a large sign that said THE PHOENIX.

This and other significant signs continued to present themselves to me, including white feathers lying on my doorstep, heart-shaped items, infinity symbols and repeated numbers that had significance for me and Robin, such as 21.09 (his birthday), which I would continually see on my phone, on receipts or as door numbers or licence plates. Whatever their source, these signs brought more than comfort. They allowed me to shake off fear. They showed me the way to navigate the most difficult time of my life. They reminded me why I am here and what I can bring to this world. They allowed me to live again and move forward in a way that would create a legacy for the person I loved so deeply, which is something I felt I had to do to carry on. They allowed me to see the wonder of life in all its technicolour glory beyond what science has already explained. And they also piqued my curiosity – what was this new clarity I had found, and could I help others to find it too? This is the purpose of the book: to share with you my newfound conviction that we all have much to gain by opening our minds to signs. This might be confirmation that you're on the right path or a comforting sense that something or someone is guiding you. And with this new source of support and external validation, you can overcome any of life's challenges and flourish like never before.

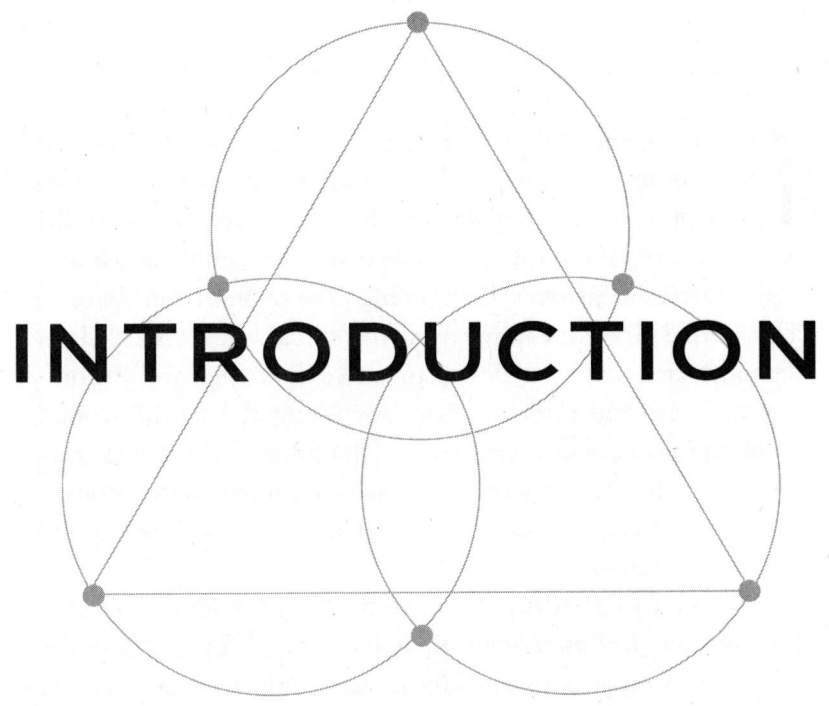

INTRODUCTION

For thousands of years, humans relied on their senses and intuition for survival. They couldn't check a weather app on their phone, but they could look at the sky, hear the wind in the trees, feel the rain on their skin, rely on their instincts and understand whether they should take shelter from a storm. They could draw meaning from the things they observed, as demonstrated by their desire to make symbolic and decorative cave art and totems – not only about the world around them, but also about their purpose, the future and what is truly important. In the modern world, with its many distractions, I believe we have lost something crucial to our well-being and ability to flourish.

A lot of us feel adrift or as if something is missing. Do you, for example, feel as though life is passing you by at 100 miles per hour? Are you consumed by anxiety or the feeling that there should be more to life? Do you dismiss anything that can't be explained rationally, even if it feels like ignoring something you know to be true in your gut? If this sounds familiar, rest assured, you are not alone. Modern life is full of stress, in large part caused by technological advancements driving us to live faster, work harder and stare at screens all day rather than looking around and seeing all that there is to guide and nourish us. As a consequence, many of us feel more lost and disconnected than we ever have before, leading to a widespread lack of direction, loss of confidence and diminished sense of purpose. This is something that I have seen in my work as a psychiatrist, neuroscientist and executive adviser, and colleagues who remain in clinical practice have described to me sharp rises in anxiety, aggressive behaviour, impatience and poor emotional regulation in their patients.

The British mental health charity Mind reports that one in four people in England will experience a mental health condition each year,[1] and the numbers of young people in particular who are facing mental health issues is on the rise, with one in six young people experiencing a mental health problem in 2020, up from one in nine in 2017.[2] Some people have also made the link between this increase in mental health issues and the increased use of smartphones and the widespread use of social media among children, particularly girls.[3] In his book *The Anxious Generation*, social psychologist Jonathan Haidt eloquently lays out the case for this in young people, but there is increasing evidence that adults are adversely affected by social media use too.[4] Smartphones are ubiquitous today, and the more time we spend staring at screens instead of looking up and noticing and engaging with the world, the more lost we will become.

It can sometimes feel as if we are stumbling from one crisis to another or perhaps not making the most of the precious time we have on this earth. There are a number of reasons for this: we live in a more material-focused world than ever before, one in which our lives are defined by consumerism, at least in the West, and the 'perfect' life is dictated to us by social media. Meanwhile, many of us have lost touch with nature in an increasingly urbanised, technological world, and thanks to individualism we have become disconnected from the idea that there is something bigger than ourselves. The increase in secularism and spirituality being downgraded by science has also left us without a source of meaning and direction that we have relied on for millennia. These factors can make it feel as though we are going through life with blinkers on by shrinking our horizons and narrowing our perception of all that the world has to offer. As such, it is hard to keep a grasp on our sense of self, on our ability to trust ourselves, and on our communities and relationships – no wonder we have seen an increase in stress, anxiety and other physical and mental illnesses. If you remove the blinkers placed on your perception by the trials and tribulations of modern living, you too can find the signs that will direct you to that deeper connection with yourself and with life.

Often our response to all of this is to try to think our way out of the problems we face, putting too much emphasis and value on rationality. However, a rational approach is not always the answer because, as I described in *The Source*, we have other ways to make decisions at our disposal, in particular our intuition, which provides us with access to knowledge and wisdom held in the body beyond our rational minds – and we can use this to find creative solutions to seemingly insurmountable issues, such as who to commit to in the long term and what we should be doing with our lives. Unfortunately, many of us are too quick to dismiss the importance of this invaluable resource. Science provides us with landmarks, but intuition can show us the gradients in between them if we tap into it more and give it at least equal billing to rationality, allowing us to make more nuanced and holistic decisions for our life. This is not to say, however, that there is no scientific basis for intuition. In recent years, the neuroscientific evidence to support the validity of intuition has come on leaps and bounds, particularly with the advances made in brain-scanning technology (more on this in Chapter 2).

Intuition has a lot to teach us. If you listen to it, your intuition has the capacity to help you understand important knowledge held in your body and subconscious, and to interpret messages that you receive from other sources, to provide you with information that could help you to see your way through challenges, look ahead with clarity and give you the understanding and strength you need to reach your goals. In particular, if you are tuned in to your intuition and able to trust what it tells you, you will be better able to notice and take advantage of your signs.

The signs that come to us are most often from unexplained sources, like the robins in my garden that I described in the Preface. Some people would call these paranormal, or make reference to the occult, but those words have pejorative connotations. I prefer to think of them as being esoteric or mystical and simply beyond our current understanding. Perhaps they come from some benevolent source that you might call God, angels or the universe, depending on your personal frame of reference, or perhaps they are from the spirits of lost loved ones who are sending us signs to help guide and comfort us. Wherever they come from, we can find many of the solutions we are seeking by looking to these signs – through having a better understanding of what our bodies and environments are telling us, and a willingness to consider the possibility of messages from powers outside of our current understanding. I will share with you the reasons why I have come to believe this and how you too can bring the benefits of signs into your life.

In the early twentieth century, psychologist Carl Jung coined the term 'synchronicity' as a way of describing what he called 'meaningful coincidences' – that is, two or more events that are seemingly connected in the absence of any causal link.[5] Despite his scientific background, Jung was open to the possibility that these synchronicities might even point to some spiritual source, something that he considered in more depth in his theory of the collective unconscious (which I discuss in Chapter 8). But regardless of whether they are coincidences or synchronicities that have a deeper source and meaning, what really matters when it comes to signs is your interpretation of what they mean to you, and the joy they can bring. The signs I saw after Robin died provided me with comfort and helped me to move forward. But although I initially used signs to help me navigate my grief, they have now become a way of life for me, helping me to feel guided by the universe, providing me with greater confidence in my intuition and making me feel more connected to nature and to other people. For you, it could be something different, as signs are personal to each individual. I want to show you in this book that there are many reasons to open your mind to the possibility that they could be real.

Have you already had something happen that you thought was a sign? As I began to share my experiences, almost everyone I spoke to about signs had a story about thinking of someone and that person suddenly messaging them or bumping into them out of the blue, and many more people than I expected had stories of sensing the presence of lost loved ones, which opened up conversations that people don't often have for fear of others thinking they are losing their minds. This made me determined not just to explore this for myself but also to legitimise this conversation in a credible and helpful way for others.

Opening Your Mind to Signs

Drawing on my own experience, the clues provided by evolutionary science about why we are the way we are and my expertise as a neuroscientist and psychiatrist, which has provided me with a deep understanding of how the brain works, in the chapters that follow, I will explain how you can transform yourself with a greater awareness and harnessing of the signs that many of us have lost sight of, to help you reconnect with yourself, with others and with life. Wherever you sit on the spectrum from sceptical to spiritual, by suspending your disbelief and extracting the lessons from my journey that are meaningful for you, I am confident you too will emerge from reading this book feeling transformed and better equipped to face life's challenges. In particular, signs can break us out of an overreliance on rationality that might not actually be serving us, and allow us a glimpse of a wider reality that provides us with a sense that we don't need to force things or worry and can trust that things will work out. This is true regardless of where you think those signs are coming from.

This book is full of practical guidance as to how you can glean the benefits from what I've learnt, including exercises that have helped me to reach another level of understanding and engagement in my day-to-day life. In Part 1, I consider the evidence for signs by investigating the possibility that the mind and body are separate. I then discuss the importance of understanding intuition and harnessing it for better decision-making more generally, and also as an interpretive tool to help you to notice and make sense of your signs. By understanding that there's a reason to listen to our intuition, we start to understand why we should pay attention to signs, too, as both are means of widening the decision-making resources available to us. I also explain why signs have been so beneficial for me and can be for you too. Finally, in Part 2, I describe ways in which you can create the conditions to welcome signs into your life via having a better understanding of your senses, an appreciation of the importance of creativity and a strong connection with nature and other people.

I've thought very carefully about the order in which to introduce you to certain topics, so I encourage you to read the book as I've laid it out; however, once you've read through from cover to cover, you can always dip back in if you need reassurance or clarification.

I would also urge you to buy a notebook or journal, if you don't already have one, and write down any observations you make as you read along, as well as record the things you start to notice about yourself and the signs you see. There will be suggestions throughout as to how to use your journal in conjunction with the book.

Grief was the catalyst for me to decide if I wanted to dwell on this tragedy that had happened to me and live with fear and bitterness, or turn it on its head and appreciate that life is way more beautiful and bigger and has more to offer if you don't just carry on in a basic, two-dimensional way. I don't, however, believe that you need to go through a major life event in order to benefit from embracing the signs that will provide you with comfort, meaning and guidance. You can choose to incorporate the lessons in this book at any time, such as to confirm that you're on the right path or to validate a decision, and by doing so enrich your experience of the world and flourish like never before.

I also want you to come away from this book with an enriched experience of the world, in which you notice and express gratitude for the beauty of everything in and around you, and see that life is more than just the day-to-day grind. In so doing, we can turn the worst times of our lives into alchemical moments that expand our consciousness and change the way we live in unbelievable ways. Opening your mind to signs is therefore a means of inviting a sense of spirituality into your life and addressing a gap that many of us have in society today. And this is what makes the lessons in this book relevant to everyone, not just those who have lost someone.

I truly believe that if you can open your mind to *your* signs, you too can live a life without limits.

PART

WHAT
ARE
YOU
MISSING?

ONE

It would have been my father's birthday recently, so my family and I visited his grave and had a dinner in his name, which was a meaningful and reflective time for us all. It made me think a lot about life, connection and the strange ways the universe weaves things together.

Speaking of which, the universe truly is a strange and mysterious place. On the train on the way to celebrate my father's life, I found myself sitting next to a woman who was reading *The Source*. I had to pause for a moment, because it felt like more than just a coincidence. I even asked if I could take a picture, and she kindly agreed. It was such a surreal, serendipitous encounter, like the universe gently nudging me with a reminder of the connections we carry with us, even when we least expect them. Not too long after, I noticed you had sent me a DM, and my mind was blown.

– Idris Blac

Unfortunately, I believe that too many of us today are missing the signs that can help to guide us towards a better life. Without them, we are ignoring a source of wisdom and knowledge that can show us the way, and also make us feel more alive and in tune with the world. This is why I want to share with you what

I've learnt about signs so that you too can take advantage of their transformative power.

In Chapter 1, I look at where signs come from, considering the possibility that they are from a source 'beyond' ourselves, whether that is lost loved ones, the universe or some other form of godhead or force. If you are going to welcome signs into your life, I believe the first step is to get a better understanding of your intuition, as without it you are much less likely to be open to receiving a sign in the first place and understanding what it means. In Chapter 2, I therefore explain why I think intuition is such a helpful interpretative tool and why you need to access and trust it more. And in Chapter 3, I look at the form these signs can take to help you recognise them in your life, and I show you how they can benefit you in meaningful ways.

CHAPTER 1

SIGNS FROM BEYOND

I n that first year after Robin's death, I was asked by filmmaker Sarah Kapoor to participate in the *Dear Me Project*,
a documentary in which she asked people from all walks of
life to pick a number ranging from 0 to 130 from a hat and
then write a short letter of a few hundred words to themselves
at that age. This exercise, which has its origins in 'writing therapy', where writing is used as a tool for healing and personal
growth, more often than not proves to be an emotive and, in
some cases, life-changing experience.[1] Sarah wanted me to discuss the neuroscience behind why this might be the case, but I
didn't want to comment only from a theoretical point of view,
so I also agreed to have a go at the exercise myself.

When it was time to film, Sarah came from Canada to visit
me in my home in London with her husband John Christensen.
They had brought me several lovely gifts, including a bottle of
maple syrup, which was Robin's favourite because he was half
Canadian. They were shocked to find out that he had passed
away, as they had been looking forward to meeting him, knowing his surname, Bieber, was a Canadian one. I showed them
some pictures of him around our house.

On the day of the interview, Sarah and I were on the sofa
together, the cameraman was off to the side and John was

watching us from across the room. Sarah asked me to pick my number from the hat and joked that John didn't like wasting paper, so he'd printed the numbers on the reverse side of a piece of paper that he'd used before. The numbers therefore randomly had the initials of people being interviewed for the documentary on the back of them – I have no idea what the original purpose of those initials was. When I picked my slip of paper, it was the number 70. It was the age that Robin would have turned that year, which made me pause for a moment, as it felt quite poignant.

When we finished the interview, I suddenly noticed that John had stood up and was overcome with emotion. I was taken aback – why was this man I hardly knew crying in my home? He then said to me through his tears, 'Turn over the piece of paper.' I'd already dropped it back in the hat, but I immediately felt a sense of urgency – a signal that I've now come to understand means a sign is imminent – and started scrabbling through the pieces of paper. I eventually found it and looked at the back, on which were printed the initials 'RB'. I started to cry too, but Sarah hadn't put it together yet and asked, 'What's going on?' John and I chimed in unison, 'Robin Bieber.' We couldn't believe it.

I kept that piece of paper, and I have the photo that John took of me holding it up not knowing what was on the other side. What are the chances? Sarah has since told me that there were 12 pieces of paper in the hat, numbered 0 to 100 in decade increments and an outlier numbered 130. She also said that the fact that 70 and RB were printed on the same piece of paper was a complete coincidence, and there actually shouldn't have been any letters on those slips of paper in the first place. The exercise wasn't about trying to receive a sign or communicate with Robin, but that was what it turned into. I believe there are certain conditions, people and places that make that more likely to happen, but more on that later.

It might be easy to dismiss my experiences of signs as coincidences or stories I told myself for comfort, if it was only me who experienced them. One case alone rarely gives us reason for further study. But since I began sharing my experiences of signs, others have opened up to me, and I now have countless stories from people I know well and people I've never met before describing their own encounters.

Rosie Wyatt reached out to me on Instagram in 2019 just after she had got divorced, and I tried to offer her some support. We exchanged a few messages that December then lost touch for a few years. She messaged me again in 2023 when her best friend Richard passed away from terminal cancer, and she had heard me briefly talk about grief on *The Diary of a CEO* podcast, which had made her sob. I tried to offer some kind words but kept it vague, as I hadn't publicly shared my own situation. But one day I felt compelled to say to her, 'You can talk to him if you work out how.' She later wrote to tell me how she had indeed managed to achieve this. As she lives close to another friend of mine, we eventually met for coffee and I told her about Robin. She now sends me the most beautiful robin poems and signs, and agreed to write this short account of her experiences:

We reconnected when Richard discovered he had cancer and returned to the UK to be near to loved ones, becoming as close as we were in those early years, perhaps even more so. His last months were filled with honesty, laughter, tears and the purest form of love. Our last moments together were tinged with emotion.

The night he died was a still May evening. I awoke to a bright flash of intense white light near my bedroom door. Keeping very still, I was aware there was no lightning or storm. At 5.30am, Richard's cousin called me to tell me he had passed before we had the chance to be with him.

A week later, I retold this unusual occurrence to another of Richard's friends. She told me that Richard had said that if he could communicate when he died, it would be through light. He'd never mentioned this to me. I have a photograph of him surrounded by fairy lights, and if I'm lost in thought, struggling with a decision or thinking of him, these lights sometimes flicker or turn off completely. Some may say this is a coincidence or happenstance, but I believe otherwise.

Once I established this more open mindset, it became easier to connect with the signs that Richard sent. Whether that's meeting people or physical signs such as light, I understand that this is a continuation of love. Richard's gift was to teach me to trust myself, and that is what I do in his memory.

Another good example came from my friend Simon, who is the cofounder of DIRTEA. The company sells functional mushrooms, and I am its chief science officer. One night, Simon had a strange dream about his former mentor, who'd passed away before his time. In the dream, Simon's mentor had led him somewhere quite sternly, saying, 'Come on, you've got to keep moving forward.' Simon phoned his mentor's widow the next day and said, 'I had this really vivid dream about your husband – it felt so real.' And she said, 'It's the one-year anniversary of his death today, and I am sure he came to check on you, as he really believed in you.' Simon had not remembered the date, but his psyche clearly had, and this encounter gave him hope that there is more to life than we know. During the dream, his heart had started racing, and he'd felt quite stressed by it, wondering if it would reoccur if he fell asleep again. In the end, however, he'd felt a level of comfort from seeing this person again and from the way his mentor's widow had responded to his experience – he described it as almost like a medicine. He'd never said anything like this to me before, but my sharing some of my experiences had encouraged him to open up about what had happened to him.

Moments like these might lead us to question – as my experience with the piece of paper did for me – whether consciousness lives on in some form after death. Could that be possible? And what evidence is there to help us understand this, one of life's biggest mysteries? This chapter explores these questions and reveals the remarkable conclusions drawn by those who have studied the moments when we are closest to death.

The Mind–Body Problem

Examples such as those from Rosie and Simon, and the many others I've collected alongside my own experiences, rest on the possibility that consciousness somehow transcends the body. This question of whether what we call the mind – or the psyche, or the self, or the soul, or any of the many other names that we use to label our subjective, first-person experience of the world – is an indivisible aspect of our physical being or a separate entity is one that has been debated by philosophers and scientists for millennia. It is also the crux of the matter when it comes to the possibility that esoteric signs could be real. If consciousness continues to exist after the death of the material body, then it could be argued that continued communication with lost loved ones would be possible.

On the face of it, the mind–body problem might not seem like much of a problem at all. In practice, on a day-to-day basis, it seems pretty obvious that our brains and minds are closely connected. However, when you delve a bit deeper, things become less clear-cut. What exactly is the nature of this relationship? If our consciousness is an emergent property of our brains, how does this work? And if our consciousness is in fact separate from our brains, how do the two things interact, such that feeling stressed can lead to us developing skin issues or watching a sad movie can cause us to cry?

These questions, and ones like them, have been pondered by some of the world's greatest minds, from Plato and Aristotle in ancient times to René Descartes in the seventeenth century right up to the modern day, with neurobiologists attempting to map brain mechanisms to subjective experiences. One branch of the debate is even referred to as the 'hard problem of consciousness', highlighting just how difficult it is to understand the relationship between the mind and body.

We don't have enough space to go into this fascinating but complex subject in great detail here. Instead, it is sufficient for our purposes to say that there are essentially two opposing ways of approaching the problem. The first is dualism, the various forms of which argue that the mind and body are ultimately separate things – for example, Descartes believed that the mind and biological matter are separate, but that the former can exert influence on the latter (although the mechanism he suggested as to how this might work has long since been shown to be inaccurate). The second is monism, which is an overarching way of describing theories that hold that seemingly opposing things arise from a single, unified source. A form of monism relevant to the mind–body problem would be materialism, which argues that physical matter is the source of all things, including seemingly immaterial things like mental states and consciousness.

There are other less well-known theories too, such as animism, which holds that all natural things, including plants, animals, rocks and weather, have spirits and can influence human events, and that the world and all its beings are part of an interconnected web. Panpsychism, meanwhile, has been put forward as a potential third option to dualism or monism. It can be summarised as the philosophical idea that consciousness is a fundamental aspect of reality and not just something that humans have. The word comes from the Greek words *pan* (all) and *psyche* (soul).

So far, neuroscience has been unable to come up with any evidence that the materialist position, which you might expect a scientist would generally lean towards, is the correct one, as the discipline has been unable to find any physical mechanism that would account for subjective experience, which is wholly intangible. Yes, it is possible to locate the part of the brain that tells us we are hungry, but it is not yet understood how that bio-chemical process is translated into an experience of hunger – in other words, what it feels like to us as individuals to be hungry. Or, to put it another way, an idea has no physical properties – it can't be touched or reduced to a physical mechanism – so how do our material bodies make them? And how can an idea in turn prompt our bodies to act?

Could it therefore be that a dualist explanation is right after all and consciousness is in fact separate from the body? Three intriguing phenomena perhaps point us in the right direction.

Near-death experiences

It is obviously extremely difficult to say what happens to our consciousness when we die, which is why faith is at the heart of all religious belief. However, we do get a tantalising glimpse into what happens after death thanks to what are known as near-death experiences (NDEs). These occur after the physical body dies but is successfully resuscitated and the patient subsequently reports having experienced consciousness during the time when they were pronounced clinically dead. The criteria for death in such cases are that the heart has stopped (cardiac arrest) and there is no detectable brain activity (as demonstrated by a flatline EEG). The sceptic might say that just because no brain activity is detectable doesn't mean that it is not happening – instead, it could be that we just don't know how to detect this activity yet.

However, by our current understanding, NDEs happen when the body is dead and no conscious activity should be possible if you subscribe to the materialist position.

The psychiatrist Dr Bruce Greyson is one of the world's foremost experts in NDEs, and he has come to some interesting conclusions about what they show, despite having been raised as an atheist and having always brought the rigour of the scientific method to bear on his research since he began studying NDEs in 1976. His meticulously vetted database includes just over 1,000 cases, and other researchers around the world have their own collections of NDEs (including Jeffrey Long, who has documented more than 5,000 cases at www.NDERF.org). It is difficult to know how many NDEs have been researched, but given the large number of studies published over the past half-century, the number could certainly be in the tens of thousands. In Dr Greyson's opinion, there is too much consistency across these experiences to doubt them, and he believes, on balance, that 'there are a lot of phenomena that suggest the brain does not create our consciousness'. To him, the fact that NDEs and terminal lucidity (more on which below) occur when the brain is not functioning well, or at all, means it cannot be causing them. Although he leaves open the possibility that it could be that the brain is responsible for these phenomena in a way that is not yet understood, everything he has learnt suggests to him that the mind and body are separate.

Although many NDEs happen outside a clinical setting, meaning the accurate monitoring of vital signs is not possible, the experiences reported in such circumstances are entirely consistent with those seen in medical environments where clinical death can be confirmed. And this points to one of the amazing things about NDEs – they are remarkably similar, whether they occurred in a hospital setting, hundreds of years ago or across the globe. People all seem to experience the same sorts of things.

Some common characteristics of NDEs include:

- thought processes becoming quicker and clearer

- intense emotions, usually of peace and well-being

- out-of-body experiences, which occur in approximately 45 per cent of NDEs[2]

- seeing things beyond the capabilities of our physical senses; for example, something that is happening in another room

- a review of a person's whole life – this is similar to the idea of someone's life flashing before their eyes when they think they are about to die

- encountering other beings, lost loved ones or deities

- entering some otherworldly, non-physical realm

- arriving at a barrier beyond which there is no turning back, and therefore choosing to or being forced to return to live again

- feeling changed for the better after physical recovery from the NDE

Dr Mary Neal, an orthopaedic spine surgeon, experienced an NDE on a kayaking trip in Chile that transformed her outlook on life. On the Netflix documentary *Surviving Death*, she said, 'I felt no pain, no fear, no panic. I felt more alive than I've ever felt. I could feel my spirit sort of peeling away from my body, and my spirit was then released up to the heavens . . . I experienced all of eternity in every second, and every second expanded into all of eternity.'

While clinically dead, she encountered beings that she could not identify but who seemed to have been significant to her life in some way, as though they were perhaps her ancestors who had died before she was alive. She also found herself following a path towards a structure that she referred to as heaven. 'At the same time,' she continued, 'I could look back at the river, where my body was still submerged under water. The group of kayakers kept trying to get to me, but they were never able to do it, and after maybe 15 minutes, they had given up rescue.'

It was approximately 30 minutes until they were able to retrieve her body and start CPR. As a doctor, she was well aware that there should have been no way to come back from this length of time without oxygen, and she remains convinced that she was physically dead. During the NDE, although she was able to see what was happening to her body, she felt compelled to keep moving towards the heavenly structure before her: 'I did not want to go back down into my body. I had a very, very physical sensation of being held and comforted and reassured that everything was fine. But the beings told me it wasn't my time. That I had more work to do on earth.'

Dr Greyson has also pointed to the fact that many people who have an NDE encounter lost loved ones who have retained some sort of consciousness that can be communicated with. In most cases, these interactions are uplifting and reassuring, with the deceased loved one reassuring the person not to worry about them. Others report estranged loved ones trying to make amends or settle old grievances.

When I spoke to Dr Greyson, I was much persuaded by one story that he told me when I asked him if he believed it was possible to communicate with deceased loved ones. Although many people who have an NDE report interacting with relatives who have died many years previously, the sceptic would say that this is wishful thinking, because most of us would welcome the opportunity to be reunited with someone we loved. The most compelling argument for our ability to communicate with people who have died therefore comes from examples in which the person having the NDE encounters someone who they did not know was dead. In the story Dr Greyson recounted to me, a patient in South Africa was suffering from respiratory arrest as a result of severe pneumonia and was having to be repeatedly resuscitated. The primary nurse involved in his care in the ICU went away for the weekend, and the patient had another arrest in which he encountered the nurse in an NDE. He couldn't understand why she was there. She told him that he had to go back to his body and asked that he apologise to her parents on her behalf for crashing the red MG. When he came round after the NDE, he was very agitated and explained what he had experienced to the nurse who had temporarily taken over his care. She ran out of the room crying, and he later found out why. His primary nurse had taken the weekend off to celebrate her twenty-first birthday and had been gifted a red MG by her parents. She had taken it out for a test drive and crashed it, dying instantly a few hours before the patient's NDE. There was no way he could have known that she was dead, let alone how she had died. This, and other remarkable stories like it, have played a major role in convincing me that my communication with Robin is not just wishful thinking.

Terminal lucidity

The phenomenon of terminal lucidity (TL) also offers potential evidence that the mind and body are separate; however, TL differs from NDEs in that it happens before someone dies and is characterised by the return of consciousness or high cognitive function in the hours or days before death in people with brain damage or severe cognitive impairment, such as dementia. TL has not yet been widely researched, so it is difficult to say how commonly it occurs; however, one retrospective study at a Korean teaching hospital found six cases out of 338 deaths. The TL lasted from a few hours up to as much as four days, and half the people died within a week and the rest within nine days.[3]

TL is frequently accompanied by a self-awareness of the phenomenon, along with an understanding of its fleeting nature. As such, people often use the experience to say goodbye, to forgive grievances or to reconnect and share memories, making it an experience that can be filled with dignity, beauty, hope and love.

One example that was described to me was of an elderly woman who'd had dementia for years and had not been able to recognise her own children, let alone her grandchildren, for most of that time, suddenly one day calling her son over by name and having a lovely conversation with him just as they had in previous years before her illness began. He felt buoyed by it and even hoped that she was somehow getting better and returning to her old self. She passed away that night.

Because cognitive function returns in people whose brains are thought to be irrevocably damaged (it is currently the medical consensus that dementia is irreversible), this suggests that 'the mind or the conscious self is not fully at the mercy of our brain', as explained to me by Professor Alexander Batthyány, who is director of the Viktor Frankl Institute and author of *Threshold*.[4] This perhaps suggests that a high-functioning mind is not necessarily contingent on or the product of a healthy and high-functioning brain after all.

Past-life memories

In most traditions that believe in reincarnation, it is not thought that the souls who are reincarnated have any knowledge of this transfer having happened. Despite this, some people do report having past-life memories, which could provide further evidence that consciousness lives on beyond the death of the physical body. Some efforts have been made within academic circles to study and substantiate these claims. In the 1950s, the psychiatrist Ian Stevenson began to look at the possibility of reincarnation as a potential explanation for certain illnesses that did not seem to be caused by either environmental or genetic factors and could perhaps therefore be attributed to some form of reincarnation. He did not ultimately commit to this position but did feel it was a plausible and perhaps even likely explanation. He was later joined at the University of Virginia School of Medicine by the child psychiatrist Jim B. Tucker, who aided him with and then took over his work on reincarnation in 2002 and who wrote *Before: Children's Memories of Past Lives*.[5] The cases they studied tended to focus on young children, as it was believed that there was less chance for these subjects to be unduly influenced by external factors or even to be coerced into lying about their past-life memories by someone acting in bad faith.

It's interesting that the research into past-life memories tends only to be done on children who are five years old and younger, because after that they might have access to information that would influence them. I think the assumption that before school and society has an impact on you, your consciousness is more open and it gets reduced later in life through education and social norms is an interesting one. And despite past-life memories seemingly having little scientific basis at the moment, they could one day be another part of the puzzle when it comes to the question of what happens to our minds after we die.

Kindred spirits

There is an interesting school of thought around soul families of kindred spirits that find each other in every incarnation of life, whether this is as friends, family or even pets. This manifests itself by you feeling drawn to these people in your life for inexplicable reasons. Write in your journal if you have ever felt like you've known someone your whole life when you first met them, or if there is someone in your social circle who you feel a deep bond with who might be in your soul family.

Although NDEs, TL and past-life memories all provide potential examples of a form of consciousness that is separate from the physical body, it is NDEs that have been studied the most and that seem to me to offer the most convincing evidence. Those who have experienced NDEs generally report that they no longer believe death to be the end of existence. Instead, they feel confident that their sense of self, identity or consciousness will in some way go on. And they do not feel the paradox of dualism – to them, it makes complete sense that they can be a conscious individual *and* connected to everything else. In other words, the possibility that a part of us endures after death cannot be ruled out.

According to Dr Eben Alexander, who wrote the bestselling book *Proof of Heaven* about his NDE while falling into a coma and suffering brain damage as a result of bacterial meningitis, and who was an atheist up until that point:

My experience showed me that the death of the body and the brain are not the end of consciousness, that human experience continues beyond the grave. More important, it continues under the gaze of a God who loves and cares about each one of us and about where the Universe itself and all the beings within it are ultimately going.[6]

In Favour of Dualism

So, if materialism doesn't explain what we observe about consciousness when we study phenomena such as NDEs and TL, where does that leave us? To me, and many others, the dualist position provides the most compelling answer. The existence of esoteric signs from lost loved ones ultimately relies on dualism, as this form of communication requires consciousness to exist separately from the physical body and therefore be able to persist in some way after death. While there is no definitive answer in sight as to whether this is correct, there are many reasons, I believe, to favour it.

For instance, I am drawn to the way in which Stanford neuroscientist David Eagleman describes how the brain and mind might operate separately. While materialism insists the mind is the by-product of brain activity, some dualists suggest that the brain is the hardware and there are signals (the software) that it picks up. Eagleman writes in his book *Incognito*: 'I'm not asserting that the brain is like a radio, but I am pointing out that it could be true. There is nothing in our current science that rules this out.'[7] Interestingly, Eagleman has also written a work of fiction called *Sum: Forty Tales from the Afterlives* about a wide variety of possible life-after-death scenarios.[8]

Then there is Donald Hoffman, an American cognitive psychologist who studies consciousness, visual perception, evolutionary psychology and the mind–body problem. He got his PhD from the brain and cognitive science department at MIT and is professor emeritus at the University of California, Irvine, but he grew up in the Christian fundamentalist church and so has been exposed to very different views about the nature of reality over the course of his life. He states that the commonly held view that brain activity causes conscious experience is difficult, if not impossible, to prove scientifically and proposes the alternative theory that consciousness rather than space–time is fundamental to existence.[9] In this model, which is underpinned by cutting-edge theoretical mathematics, it is consciousness that causes brain activity and, in fact, all the objects and properties of the physical world. This is obviously an extremely challenging thing to wrap your head around. Thankfully, it is not necessary to delve deeper here, but it does point to the fact that credible alternative explanations to the mind–body problem exist. The possibility of challenging the current paradigm with these kinds of open-minded ideas excites me as a scientist who is also searching for answers to the mysteries of the human condition.

Additionally, although the prioritisation of science and rationality means that materialism is the predominant philosophy today, it hasn't always been that way. It wasn't until the Enlightenment and the rise of modern science that the materialist view took precedence. For most of human existence, dualism has been the default position, as it is the cornerstone of all major religions and underpins the belief systems of most ancient civilisations.

I was brought up in a household in which reincarnation was taken to be a fact of life, as demonstrated by my father believing that I was a reincarnation of my grandmother. The Hindu belief in reincarnation is referred to in Sanskrit as *saṃsāra*, in which the soul or *Ātman*, which is distinct from the physical body, is continually reborn into heaven, hell or back on earth in a living being, which can be an animal or a human. *Karma* accrued in life dictates the nature of this rebirth, and no state is permanent, with every soul, whether it was in heaven or in the body of an animal, eventually being reincarnated back on earth. This endless cycle is generally seen to be something from which the soul wishes to break free by achieving *moksha*, a state of grace equivalent to or identical with *Brahman*, which is the ultimate reality of the universe, sometimes referred to as *Sat-cit-ānanda* (truth-consciousness-bliss). Hindu scriptures such as the *Upanishads* and *Bhagavad Gita* focus on how one might attain *moksha*. Sikh theories of reincarnation have much in common with Hindu ones, subscribing to the same endless cycle of *saṃsāra*, but in their doctrines it is the grace of God that liberates the soul.

Reincarnation is also central to Buddhism, but the concept of a soul is different in that tradition. Buddhist doctrines hold that there is no permanent spirit or self. Instead, there is one universal consciousness, and *nirvana* is achieved when an individual mind can let go of the self and ego and recognise the impermanence of everything. Similarly to Hinduism, the endless cycle of reincarnation is equated with suffering, or *duḥkha*, and the ultimate goal is salvation and liberation from earthly attachment.

The dualist position does not just underpin religions that developed in the East. Although the big three monotheistic religions of Christianity, Judaism and Islam ultimately diverged and spawned many different sects, they all stem from the same source and therefore share fundamental beliefs. First and foremost, they all believe in the existence of a soul that is separate from the body and that on death will be judged or made to reflect on its actions during its life before being admitted to some sort of heaven-like realm, or condemned to hell or its equivalent if it is considered to be irredeemable. The concept of resurrection plays a part in all three religions, too. The resurrection of Jesus is, of course, a central tenet of Christianity, and all three Abrahamic traditions believe in a Judgement Day or second coming when nearly all people who have lived will be resurrected to live again. All of these beliefs rest on the idea that the soul or spirit is immortal and survives the death of the body.

The concepts of souls and an afterlife can be seen across most ancient cultures too. Today, we know of at least 1,500 deities worshipped by the Ancient Egyptians, which provide us with our earliest records of spiritual and religious beliefs.

We also know that they believed in a soul or life force that was separate from the body and persisted beyond death, and which was made up of two main elements. The *ka*, the vital essence of a living person, was thought to leave the body at the time of death. Because the *ka* was sustained in life by food and drink, provisions would be left in tombs so that it would have what it needed to survive in death. The *ba*, meanwhile, was the part of the soul that represented everything that made each individual unique, almost like what we would refer to as 'personality'. The *ba* was thought to maintain a connection with the body after death, and funeral rites were performed to allow it to separate from the body and join with the *ka* to create an *akh*, which could be described as the intellect as a living entity. The *ba* was believed to return to the body each night to be refortified before joining with the *ka* to form an *akh* the next day. This was why the body was mummified and placed in a tomb.

Although these beliefs might seem fantastical to us today, they rely on the same dualist principles as nearly all other recorded religions and belief systems since then, demonstrating that the separation of body and mind has in many ways always been the most intuitive answer that humans have come up with to make sense of life and death. That was certainly the case with the Ancient Greeks and Romans as well. In Greek mythology, the god Hades was king of the underworld, where a soul would go when its host body died. This belief system persisted into Roman times, where it evolved and developed further. Hades became known as Pluto, and in the Roman poet Virgil's *Aeneid*, many of the same features of the afterlife central to Greek mythology can be seen, including the River Styx and the blissful fields of Elysium.

Ethnic, or pagan, religions in Europe before Christianity tended to be polytheistic (worshipping more than one god or deity) and, again, the concepts of souls and an afterlife were central to most of them. In Norse paganism, for example, a range of beliefs about what happened after death were prevalent, with multiple possible destinations for a soul, including Odin's Valhalla, where the warrior elite who had died in battle would reside, and Hel for those who had died of natural causes.

Polytheism was not only to be found in Europe. The Mayan civilisations of Mesoamerica (modern-day central and southern Mexico, all of Belize, Guatemala and El Salvador, and parts of Honduras, Nicaragua and Costa Rica) believed that the soul was connected to the body at birth and that only sickness or death could separate them. It was also widely held that it was possible to communicate with deceased ancestors, and many Mayan rituals and spiritual practices revolved around looking to lost loved ones for advice and guidance.

I could list many more examples: Australian Aboriginal culture, the Māori culture of New Zealand, the Inca culture of South America, and so on. The point is that for most of human history, and presumably dating to prehistoric times, humans believed in the separation of the mind and body and of the continuation of the self after death. We could look back from our position of supposed technological and scientific superiority in the twenty-first century and argue that they just didn't know any better, because they hadn't yet made the discoveries that we now have, but this misses the point. There is no more concrete evidence for a materialist position today than there is for a dualist answer to the mind–body problem. And I would in fact argue that there is more compelling evidence that consciousness is not simply a by-product of our physical matter.

It seems that times of extreme duress, such as at the border of life and death, perhaps expose what is always the case – that the mind and body can operate separately. However, I believe we can glimpse this reality in everyday life too via nature, creativity, meditation, breathwork, psychedelics, dancing and drumming.

It's about putting your nervous system into a state of openness. We lose control fully during an NDE, but we can approximate this experience by creating the conditions to let go a little bit, and this may begin with letting go of what we rationally believe to be true. If we can do this, and open our minds to signs, we can find a greater purpose in life. A useful step on the journey to that point is to rely more on your intuition, which I discuss in more detail in the next chapter.

KEY TAKEAWAYS

1. There is much to be learnt about the nature of consciousness from the science of the border of life and death, and the spirituality of ancient cultures.
2. The mind is capable of more than the brain allows in the material world – something you can learn to expand.
3. The argument that consciousness lives on means that you can receive signs from beyond if you allow yourself to notice them.

CHAPTER 2

ARE YOU ACCESSING YOUR FULL WISDOM?

n 1998, during my penultimate year at medical school, I went to Cape Town for work experience, and I met Fritz, who would become my first husband. A year after we met, I visited him in South Africa and he decided to introduce me to his parents. The night before we were due to begin our 20-hour car journey to see them, I had a dream that I was in their house, and both of his brothers, his sister and their mother were sitting around and crying, and Fritz's father was walking around behind everyone saying, 'Everything's fine. Everything's going to be okay. Don't cry. Don't be sad.' In the dream, I was the only one who could see or hear him – Fritz and his family couldn't.

I initially attributed this dream to my feeling anxious about meeting Fritz's parents, but later that day we received the news that his father had suddenly passed away. Could the dream have been a premonition, or someone trying to tell me that his spirit would live on to console his family? Perhaps, but I didn't question it too much at the time, and I didn't discuss it with Fritz, as I thought it would be too upsetting for him. In retrospect, I have now come to view this seemingly prophetic dream as an example of precognition and hidden wisdom, which are extended forms of intuition, and a source of knowledge and information that I didn't know I had at that age and wasn't accessing at that time in a deliberate way. In the years following this dream, I slowly but surely began to recognise the importance of hidden wisdom, in particular intuition, which I have come to rely on so much to help show me the best way forward, and also to help me notice and understand my signs.

Harnessing the Brain's Filtering System

The reality is, we are constantly filtering information and missing things that could be useful to us. The reason for this is that the brain has evolved to be as efficient as possible, and it therefore creates shortcuts. We can see the way the brain filters out information that it deems unnecessary by looking at the ascending reticular activating system (ARAS). This is a non-conscious process that selects what we need to pay attention to. Think of the nursing mother who sleeps through a car alarm in the street but wakes as soon as she hears her baby cry, or the fact that you're not aware of the clothes on your body all day, because that would be a huge amount of data from your skin, which is your largest organ, for your brain to process. It's not essential information to our survival, so it can quite easily be filtered out. We can learn to override this filtering process through mindful intervention and better priming of our brains to notice what it might otherwise have missed (this is something that I will discuss in more detail later, as it is central to our ability to notice and take advantage of signs).

We can also get a glimpse of this relaxation of the ARAS when we are dreaming. In order to fall asleep, you generally have to be in a place of physical and psychological safety, so there is less need for the brain to prioritise only what is critical to your survival. Being relaxed sometimes leads to apparent communication with unknown sources or access to otherwise hidden information. This helps to explain the seemingly prophetic dreams that I and others have experienced. Dr Nida

Chenagtsang, a Tibetan doctor and philosopher, says that deep sleep is a profound meditative state that is akin to an NDE. When we get lost in a dream, it is as if we are in another world and not mentally present in this one, making each night like a mini death experience. So, signs may also come to us in our dreams (more on which later).

Selective attention and filtering are examples of the brain's saliency network, which helps us to focus on the sensory data that is most relevant to our survival. You can't pay attention to everything around you, because if you did, you wouldn't be able to function, like in the example of not being aware of the feeling of clothes on your body.

Salience in neuroscientific terms is the process by which an organism's brain non-consciously directs its limited perceptual and cognitive resources to notice what it considers to be most important or pertinent. It is the opposite of habituation, which is the process by which the brain begins to remove its perceptual resources from noticing things that it is repeatedly exposed to and therefore deems unimportant. Even if something is really amazing, like a building or a tree, if you walk past it every day, eventually it doesn't create saliency or grab your attention, because you have become used to it – that is, you have become habituated.

Salience works in a variety of ways:

- novelty – perceiving something new or unusual will have a greater impact on your brain

- filtering – as in the case of the ARAS, how much you direct your attention to what you feel passionate about will have an impact on what will be filtered

- selective attention – the process by which the brain focuses on what it deems important and ignores what it considers to be distractions

- value tagging – your brain has a natural ranking for the importance of the things that you pay attention to. There are two elements to this: a logical one, which is very much related to survival, and an emotional one, which is more about thriving

In practice, if you notice something surprising, or if you have decided to pay attention to something, the brain non-consciously prioritises that information. For example, when people buy a new car, they often report that they then see the same model on the roads much more. There are not, of course, more of the same car around – their brains have just been primed to notice them. This process is sometimes referred to as the Baader–Meinhof phenomenon and was later labelled the 'frequency illusion' by the linguist Arnold Zwicky.[1] It is often exploited by marketers, who can use it to make us think that a product is more popular than it actually is and therefore encourage us to buy it.[2]

The filtering and value tagging that occur as the brain assigns salience are non-conscious processes that go on in the background unless you make efforts to influence and direct them. This is how action boards work: if you collect and regularly look at images of things that you want, you are more likely to notice opportunities in the real world that can bring those things into your life.

The brain also prunes disused connections and synapses, especially in the teenage years as it develops and matures, although it is now understood that this process continues into our twenties,[3] and perhaps even beyond into later adulthood.[4] In my work, I have found that if you focus on things like gratitude, beauty and happiness, rather than telling yourself that you're not worthy or that good things don't happen to you, those negative pathways are pruned, allowing you to bolster the beneficial ones.

You can't undo what's in the brain, but you can overwrite it. To improve your brain, you therefore have to overwrite the neural pathways that you don't want with new alternatives. So, if you had a feeling of not being worthy, you wouldn't work on getting rid of it; you'd work on replacing it with how you *do* want to feel, and with repetition mostly, and also with emotional intensity, that pathway would eventually overtake the old one. This is because repetition, like practising the piano, and things that have a significant emotional impact on you are embedded more strongly in the brain. This is why people who go on reality TV shows and experience heightened and intense situations often bond quickly and tell one another that they will be friends for life.

This means there is agency here. You can choose the things that you want your brain to focus on and, through repetition, positive reinforcement and affirmation, you're naturally going to prune the things that are less desirable or beneficial, just like pruning a rose bush helps new stems and buds to flourish. In this way, being curious, playful and motivated to learn new things opens you up to the benefits of saliency, whereby you can direct your attention with intentionality to the things that have meaning for you. This is especially helpful if you are feeling stressed, as stress can cloud your intuition and make you less able to notice and interpret signs (as discussed in more detail in Chapters 4 and 5).

If you are taking control of your perception, then you will be more able to notice signs. The art of noticing is a very important skill to cultivate and, combined with an abundant mindset, will allow you to bring in signs and interpret them via your intuition. The brain has a negative bias towards risk aversion as a survival mechanism, and we are more likely to choose the option that avoids loss than gains a reward. As the Nobel Prize-winning psychologist Daniel Kahneman put it, 'Organisms that treat threats as more urgent than opportunities have a better chance to survive and reproduce.'[5] In the modern world, in which our daily safety is much more assured, having an abundant mindset is a deliberate effort to overcome this outdated bias, helping us to thrive rather than just survive.

I display beautifully illustrated affirmations on cards around my house that speak to the life I desire and help to bolster the mindset that serves me best at any given moment. If you're not being proactive and directing your brain's attention to the things you really value, you're not really in control of it to the same degree as you could be. This diminishes your engagement with the world, and also potentially limits your ability to see other signs that could be beneficial to you.

Logic versus Intuition

With limited sources of information at their disposal, our ancestors had to rely much more on what their bodies were telling them, both when it came to their physical and mental well-being, and in terms of the decisions that they needed to make in order to survive. Although it is difficult to know to what extent early humans used their intuition specifically, academics such as archaeologist Steven Mithen have developed models that aim to understand decision-making behaviour among hunter-gatherers.[6] Building on this research, it seems safe to assume that they used their mind–body connection to process thoughts, feelings and emotions – for example, via some of their rituals in which they chanted or danced – to adapt to their environments in order to maximise their chances of survival, to feel grounded and connected to the earth, and to feel connected to their immediate tribe members and ancestors. Today, many of us have become very sedentary, preferring to curl up on a comfortable sofa and watch TV than get more in touch with our bodies. This disconnection from our physical selves is to the detriment of our intuition and our ability to take advantage of our signs more generally.

Prior to 2018, many of the businesspeople I advised – for example, in my work as a senior adviser for neuroscience and leadership at MIT Sloan – dismissed intuition, questioning its validity and tangibility. Most of them were happy to rely on their logic and the working memory of their cortex, but they were not willing to make important decisions, such as who to hire or fire, based on intuition. Many of them questioned if it even existed in the first place. However, as we've been able to scan brains and learn more about how neurons connect up and store information, the validity of intuition has increased. For example, imaging has shown that the orbitofrontal cortex area of the brain plays a key role in processing incomplete internal and external information in a non-conscious way, which feels to us like gut instinct.[7]

I now see more leaders, particularly the older generation, saying that intuition is absolutely the main way that they make their most important decisions, because they have learnt this through experience. This is the value of wisdom from experience, and very much the case in my own life too, as I have actively worked to improve and trust this way of thinking. I have found it to be an invaluable way of choosing which path to take, and it has also allowed me to notice and interpret signs that have helped me through the toughest times, and to find renewed purpose and optimism.

Despite the fact that I have seen intuition become more widely accepted as a decision-making tool in business circles over the past few years, getting closer to how it has been valued in other parts of society, particularly the more creative or spiritual parts, which have always valued intuition, many of us are still not accessing this invaluable resource effectively enough ... or at all. Some of this comes down to the prioritisation in modern life of data and rationality, like tracking our sleep but not listening to our bodies when we are tired; taking food intolerance tests instead of recognising which foods make us feel bloated or sluggish; and following trends like high-intensity exercise, which can actually be counterproductive if it doesn't suit your metabolism. However, this logical approach is restrictive, as our brains are not our only source of information – our bodies hold knowledge too (which I discuss in more detail in Chapter 4). The everyday pressures of modern life also lead us to lose sight of our embodied intuition in favour of a more rational approach to the decisions we make – it is all too easy to look for the app or quick fix that is going to make our lives easier and tell us what to do. I know that when I am feeling overwhelmed, I just want someone or something to direct me. However, we can't outsource our decision-making, and influencers on social media, for example, are not going to provide us with the answers we need. Instead, accessing our minds and bodies together can unlock a whole new level of knowledge and intuitive insight that can guide us in the right direction.

It's also worth noting that until the age of at least 18, it's quite hard to be intuitive, because you just don't have sufficient life experience to draw on. When I've coached younger people, I've seen that they haven't had enough scenarios repeat in their lives to use that knowledge to make decisions and change direction. This is why journalling and reading back over the entries is so important to honing your intuition, particularly when you are younger. Sometimes I read things in my journal that I had completely forgotten about, so those could have become lost learning opportunities.

Insights from your dreams

I urge you to grab your journal and pen right now and start recording your dreams, dilemmas and any insights from your intuition.

There are no hard-and-fast rules when it comes to journalling, but you can record the events of your day and the emotions associated with them, write about how you made an important decision and then later return to it to see how things panned out. Or you can make a note of times when your body sent you a message, such as via goosebumps. The earlier you start this, the better, because you can hone your intuition with practice, although it's also never too late to start. If you try to begin accessing your intuition when you're younger, you're more likely to build it into something you really feel you can rely on.

Accessing Your Intuition

To access your intuition most effectively, a combination of the emotional and the physical is required. The emotional centres are deep inside the brain in the limbic system, which is an area about the size of your clenched fist proportional to your body. Around that is the cortex, which has more of the logical pathways of the brain. It is believed that this is where we keep our working memory, such as the things we need to remember to do our jobs and go about our everyday lives. All memories are created through a process called Hebbian learning, which is named after the neuroscientist Donald Hebb – this mechanism is most simply explained by the idea that neurons that fire together wire together.[8] The more we do something, whether it's learning a language or accessing our intuition, stronger and deeper connections are forged between nerve cells, which allows electrical and chemical signals to pass between them more easily. A good analogy for this is walking through a field of tall grass. The first time you walk through it, you have to take high steps and push the grass down, and that's difficult. However, if you walk along that path every day, the grass gets flatter and flatter, and it becomes much easier. Eventually, you can get to the point where you can put down some paving stones and make it a really solid, permanent pathway. That's what happens in your brain when you learn something.

You can't, of course, consciously remember everything that you've experienced in your whole life, but it has all had an impression on your brain–body system. It is therefore believed that our wisdom and pattern recognition get pushed deeper and deeper into the emotional centre of the brain and on into the spinal cord, and even into our gut neurons and possibly fascia.* This means that our psychological experiences leave a physical imprint, as discussed by Bessel van der Kolk in his seminal book *The Body Keeps the Score* (which I discuss in more detail later in the book).[9] As it stands, we don't fully understand how that physical imprint is generated, but we do know that our cells are impacted by our experiences and change our physiology through the process of epigenetics.[10] This points to the store of information at a non-conscious, cellular level.

Many of the lessons that you've picked up in life, and much of the wisdom that you've learnt through repeated patterns, are held deep down in your gut. That's why intuition is some-times called 'gut instinct'. This phrase came before the science confirmed it, so people clearly already had an inkling that this

---

* Fascia was once believed to be nothing more than connective tissue that holds things together in the body and it would be cut away with-out a thought in surgery. However, there is now growing evidence that it performs an important function in the body, providing stabilisation, con-nection and support for our organs, muscles, nerves and blood vessels. It also has sensitive nerve endings, and it can tighten up when we are under stress, which is why it is the basis of a lot of healing massage therapies, going beyond the tension in our muscles and joints, and digging deeper into our fascial tissue.

was where intuition was potentially coming from. Furthermore, it is now believed that in response to certain life experiences, we hold bracing patterns that show up in our musculature and fascia; for example, if you are stressed out, you might find that you hunch over more or clench your fists, and these bracing patterns can become ingrained in our bodies.

As with trauma, wisdom and hidden information can also be stored in cells in your body via Hebbian learning. You're not conscious of this store of wisdom, but it's still a valuable guide to the decisions that you make, as well as a means of extracting meaning from the signs that you receive.

The interconnection between signs and intuition

I know intuition is something that has been incredibly valuable to me in terms of the way I have lived my life. In fact, as I mentioned, I have come to think of intuition as my superpower. It became central to how I made decisions after I got divorced in my mid-thirties, when I started journalling and making action boards, but I was already using it before then. For example, when I was a junior doctor, I remember treating one patient on the ward who suddenly got a terrible nosebleed. I called my registrar and, when I told him what was happening, he said, 'It's a nosebleed. I think you can deal with it.' I said okay and tried to do a bit more, but it was gushing and wouldn't stop. Deep down, I just knew something wasn't right, so I trusted my intuition and called the registrar back and said, 'Look, this is the worst nosebleed I've ever seen.' A few minutes later, he sauntered up. Upon seeing the level of haemorrhaging, he became quite alarmed and tried to staunch the nosebleed himself. He wasn't able to either, so, in the end, we had to call the ear, nose and throat specialist, who performed an emergency procedure with equipment that was not available on our ward. I dread to think how it might have turned out if I had hesitated to call for help out of some false sense of pride, and it was a useful lesson that I should trust my intuition more.

Over time, putting more stock in my intuition has paid off, to the point that it now plays an integral role in my ability to take advantage of my signs. This is something that I know other people have found too. A good example of someone trusting their intuition and this allowing her to see a sign that helped guide and comfort her was given to me by Mimi Zouch, a painter, sculptor and entrepreneur:

As a single woman in her forties with my own business as an artist and a day job in law, I had a pretty busy life, but I was yearning for the next exciting chapter. I was ready to find a life partner and to pour my energy and soul into my passion – my art – but it felt impossible to step away from the security of a well-paid job. I'd been struggling with my mental health from corporate burnout for some time, and I needed a break, so when my good friend announced a couple of weeks before Christmas 2024 that she'd booked flights to Sri Lanka for the New Year, I knew in my gut I just had to go too.

I made some wonderful new friends on the trip and was having a fabulous time, but had not had the holiday romance I'd hoped for. Three days before coming home, I returned after dinner to the beautiful cabana I was staying in. It was dark, but there, shining in the porch light, I could see a little creature right in front of my door that I'd never seen before – a beautiful praying mantis. It was doing a dance with its arms from side to side. I quickly took a film of it to capture the moment before gently moving it out the way and heading into my room.

The next day over dinner I was retelling this story to my friends, and they explained that seeing a praying mantis is a sign you will come into good fortune, especially if you see it on your doorstep. I was delighted by this and knew it was a sign. Later that evening, at a party, my friend pointed out a handsome man standing on his own under a coconut tree . . . he turned out to be my holiday romance for the last two days of my trip. Then, a couple of days later in the airport, for the first time ever on a long-haul flight, I was upgraded to business class.

I came home with a totally fresh mindset and knowing I was in charge of my life. I also knew more good fortune was heading my way. Then, just 12 days after my return, I was told that after almost 18 years working in the same company, I was being made redundant. For most people, this would have been devastating news, but for me it was the shove I had been waiting for. I realised that now was my time to shine, and I can't wait to see what other good fortune lies ahead for me.

Can you think of instances in your own life when you have trusted your intuition? And have these moments been linked to or led to signs? If you begin to journal more regularly, you might be able to see connections between your intuition and signs that you might not otherwise have made, and this will help you to be more aware of the possibility in the future.

Listening to your intuition is not just a way to reconnect with how our ancestors made decisions and expand the breadth of knowledge available to you, it is also a vital component when it comes to noticing and understanding signs. Later in the book (in Chapters 4 and 5), I will explain how you can raise your awareness of the world and quieten the noise of modern life so you can make full use of your intuition. First, though, I want to show you why I believe signs to be so beneficial and suggest ways in which you can begin to welcome them into your life.

KEY TAKEAWAYS

1. You can prime your brain to notice signs.
2. You can hone your intuition through mind and body to create a superpower.
3. Intuition and signs are connected.

CHAPTER 3

LIFE WITH SIGNS

In a moment of serendipity, I became friends with a taxi driver called Roony who I had interacted with on Instagram, after which he had randomly picked me up in his cab one day. When I heard that his grandmother was a medium, I was gripped by this feeling that I had to meet her and have a reading from her, so I accepted an invitation to go to her house with Roony. His mum was there too and, after chatting for about an hour, she said, 'Are you married?' I replied, 'Before I answer that question, I would love to get a reading.' So, his grandmother and I went upstairs to her 'special' room.

To begin with, she asked me for an object, as she said she needed something to hold on to, so I gave her my wedding ring. She asked me if it had always been mine, and I replied yes. Despite this, she initially spent quite a bit of time talking about my grandmother, which I found a bit frustrating, as I was hoping to hear from Robin. Then, suddenly, she said, 'Oh, is there someone called Rob?' I almost fell off my chair. Before I could tell her who he was, she said some things that there is absolutely no way she could have known, as they were so private and personal. These messages from Robin via the medium were another form of sign from beyond that helped comfort me and show me I was right to be welcoming signs into my life.

What she went on to tell me was confirmation of the things I had been feeling and experiencing. By this point, I had opened my mind fully to signs and raised my awareness to the point that I received them on an almost daily basis. They now help me to understand and guide me towards my purpose, and I strongly believe that they can do the same for you. This chapter looks at how you can recognise your signs and how they could change your life.

The Benefits of Signs

I once asked someone what he thought was more comforting: believing that when someone dies that's it, they're gone for ever, or believing that the spirit lives on and there might be ways you can communicate with that person and ask for signs from them. He immediately responded that the latter would provide a more hopeful and joyful way of approaching the death of those closest to you. This is certainly one of the main reasons that signs have become such a central part of my life. Feeling as though your lost loved one is not gone for ever, and that there are potentially means of communicating with them, provides real solace and comfort in the face of overwhelming grief.

At the same time, my belief in signs provides similar benefits as those described by people who have had NDEs. Their brush with a greater power and the sense that their journey will continue after life make them feel less afraid of death and more willing to take healthy risks in life, as they feel protected by something bigger than themselves. Feeling as though my connection with Robin has endured beyond his death makes me want to live to the fullest and create a legacy for the precious time we spent together. And it has removed doubt and increased my trust in myself and the way I live my life more generally.

I am not the only one who can see the benefits of signs as a means of helping us to make decisions and see a way forward. Jemma Amos is a filmmaker who I met once for a coffee and to do some filming:

> Whenever I don't know what decision to make, when I feel lost or stuck or deep in grief, my mum always says, 'Ask for an unmistakeable sign.' These signs have come in so many forms over the years. Sometimes it's words from a stranger or undeniable coincidences that can only really be described as mini miracles: songs coming on in cafés with the exact words I need to hear; white feathers appearing in places I have no idea how they got there; chance meetings in places I'd never expect. It's as though there's some other language the universe is speaking that shows itself only when we start paying attention.
>
> My mum had an experience where she was looking to buy a new house, having not moved since my dad had passed away, or even having made any sort of big decision without him. She searched for three years, but walked out of most houses within a few minutes with a firm no. There was one particular place she kept refusing to see because she didn't want to live in that part of London, but her estate agent finally convinced her, and when we were on our way, she said, as she always does, 'Please give me an unmistakeable sign of what I need to do next.' She walked into the house and the first thing she saw was a saddle, bridle and horse-riding boots in the entrance, which was quite unusual in a London home! My sister is a professional horse rider, and my mum has always been around horses, so horses are a huge sign for her. Within five minutes, she asked to start negotiations, as she knew it was her new home. She's lived there for seven years now, and her neighbours have become some of her closest friends.

You too can ask for signs to help you make important decisions about your life in any situation in which you need guidance or validation. When we're stressed or unsure, we are more likely to look for someone to tell us what to do, but signs help us to build our self-trust in our own decisions.

There will naturally be times when you're more present in the material world and not relying on signs so much. And then there'll be times when you're seeing lots of signs and going down a more spiritual path. Inevitably, people will have moments of self-doubt, but if you turn to your signs, the plasticity of the brain means that you can move away from that mode of thinking and more towards the harmony stage where you are achieving what you want and are confident in yourself. When I know that I've got lots of signs around me at any given time, I believe that correlates with me being the best version of myself that I can be in any given moment.

Signs also help you to feel more alive and more in tune with the world, rather than having a narrow, limiting perspective. Opening yourself up to the possibility of signs from what some cultures call 'beyond the veil' broadens your horizons and helps you to see the world as a place of infinite possibilities rather than one of limitations. Letting go of rigid rationality and acknowledging that there are things that you do not know and that cannot be explained promotes flexible thinking and encourages you to approach your life in a more holistic way. It also encourages you to trust yourself more and lean on your intuition.

As someone who's professionally interested in cognitive science, believing that I'm now capable of something I never thought possible is beneficial in and of itself. I never want to stop learning and growing. Signs make me feel like I'm widening my horizons. It all goes back to my professional focus on neuroplasticity and the potential of the human brain to rewire itself. For example, I love trying new foods – there's a sort of wonder in discovering something that I didn't know existed. Accessing signs feels like learning a new language for me – it's a whole new skill set that I didn't even know was possible. Everybody is capable of taking advantage of those skills, if only you know how to read them.

Finding your purpose

Finding your purpose via signs is one of the main gifts that I want you to take away from this book. And by purpose I mean having a strong sense of why you were put on this earth and following what you then know to be the right path. It is the opposite of being lost, lonely and disconnected. Having a *raison d'être* is what makes life meaningful rather than directionless. And it is a virtuous circle: you start by following signs to find your purpose, but the more you connect with your purpose, the more signs become important and present as part of your life, and all of this can have a positive impact on those around you.

This is key because in order to have the maximum well-being, it's not enough to sleep, eat well and exercise, you also need to have a purpose, including one that transcends yourself; for example, being in the service of others (which I discuss in more detail in Chapter 8). If you don't have anything to work towards, and if everything that you want out of life is to do with benefiting yourself, there is a hollowness to your experience of life. A strong sense of connection to yourself, through mind–body alignment and your powers of intuition; the benefits of art, beauty, creativity and nature; and substantial and uplifting connections with others, as well as feeling a deeper connectedness with humanity in general, are all ways of recognising signs that will lead to greater meaning and purpose, making life feel richer. In turn, signs give you that sense of connection with yourself, with others and with the universe, and this, in and of itself, provides you with purpose, which is essential for your well-being. In this way, signs are the gateway to something bigger.

The psychologist Carol Ryff came up with a model that says there are six key factors that contribute to psychological well-being, one of which is a feeling of purpose and meaning in life.[1] You could be financially successful and physically healthy, but that doesn't necessarily mean that you will feel whole, or complete, or fulfilled. You need to have purpose. A good example of this can be seen in the documentary *Live to 100: Secrets of the Blue Zones*, in which it is shown that a major component of longevity is people having a strong purpose in their family or community – babysitting or gardening, for example – even if they are 100 years old.[2]

Acknowledging that there is something bigger than ourselves can also provide a sense of purpose. If you have that frame of mind, you might be more open to trying to interpret things around you that could contribute to that sense of belonging and connectedness, and further boost your sense of purpose, one that connects you to something bigger than yourself, to a wider world and a multilayered experience of life. A greater sense of purpose takes you out of yourself, and your contribution gives back to the collective. If you are selfish in your focus, you see the world in a narrow, two-dimensional way. Altruism, on the other hand, leads to open-mindedness.

I believe that trusting in your signs provides a sense of conviction that can give you greater purpose or allow you to find it in the first place. They show you that you're on the right path and help you to re-evaluate things if need be. It's about being thoughtful about where you are in life and identifying what is important that can guide you.

A new perspective

In Chapter 1, we discussed how NDEs in particular point to the potential separation of body and mind. However, the experience itself also reveals something important about transcendent or spiritual engagement. Having an NDE seems to have a remarkable effect on people, with the overwhelming majority saying that they found the experience to be positive and life-changing, just as Dr Neal did. As such, an NDE can permanently transform a person's attitudes, beliefs, values and behaviours.

Dr Greyson said at the end of his book *After* that people who have had NDEs emerge with a greater gusto for life because they no longer fear death.[3] They also tend to be more compassionate and grateful for what they have, and more likely to embrace life with confidence and take healthy risks, as they no longer have a fear of failing. This increased value on life means they are also more likely to take advantage of its opportunities, and while they enjoy things, they are less likely to become addicted to them.

The benefits of NDEs do not stop at the level of positive individual traits. People report an increased sense of spirituality, although this does not equate with religiosity. Instead, there is a sense of intense connection to all other living beings, to the natural world and to the universe, along with an ability to commune with the divine, in whatever guise that takes. Although people often find it difficult to put their experiences into words, and frequently, in fact, say that words are insufficient to describe what they have gone through and seen, they almost always describe a warm, loving light that many name as God. This doesn't tend to be the interventionist God of the Abrahamic religions so much as a benevolent force or power that links everything together. One of the commonly reported metaphors is that the person felt like a wave in a great ocean. There is also typically a decrease in concern about material, worldly goods and matters, such as personal possessions, wealth, power, prestige and fame, coupled with an increase in selflessness and altruism.

Altered states of consciousness (ASC) can induce many of the same experiences as NDEs, and many cultures and spiritual traditions include practices that allow you to access the same benefits, such as prayer, meditation, ascetic practices (such as sensory deprivation, including fasting and social isolation), drumming, singing, dancing and the use of psychedelic substances. These techniques are ultimately not as impactful as an NDE, because you do not let go to the same degree, and the brain's filter is not dialled down as much. As a result, there is still some attempt to control the process, which is absent during an NDE, when there tends to be a complete sense of powerlessness, although this usually leads to a feeling of peace and safety in the face of the benevolent universe rather than fear or dread.

Dark retreats are probably the most similar to an NDE and arguably have the biggest impact. With their origins in Tibetan Buddhism and its close cousin Bön, which is the indigenous religion of Tibet, dark retreats consist of spending extended time in spaces in which there is no light. Yogis use them in order to see deities, but they are also becoming more widespread in secular practice as an advanced form of meditation and mindfulness that allows the individual to enter an altered state of consciousness and glimpse at first hand the separation of mind and body. One study showed that participants scored higher in terms of meaning of life, mindfulness and self-esteem following a week-long stay in a dark retreat.[4] There are also precedents from other cultures. The Ancient Greeks, for example, used sensory deprivation for divine inspiration, with seers and oracles provoking ASC in caves where no light could penetrate.[5]

During the retreat, you sit in the pitch dark and focus on your breath or on simple visualisations. People tend to sleep a lot at first, because our melatonin levels increase when there is no light. You fall asleep in darkness and wake to darkness, which leads to extremely vivid dreams. Then, in the waking state, you start to see light. At first, this might just be a flicker or two, but then the walls appear as a form of light, and people become able to reorganise reality and function in this space. These lights progress to something akin to shooting stars and can take the form of animals (normal or mystical) and eventually Buddhas or deities (similar to what Dr Greyson described). Sounds may be experienced too, but both they and the lights are all essentially hallucinations. Dark retreats are very much like lucid dreaming (where you know you are dreaming and can exert some level of control over what you see), and both have similarities to NDEs. In this way, dark retreats and the act of falling asleep and dreaming are forms of death and rebirth. As Jamie Wheal says in his book *Recapture the Rapture*, death/rebirth rituals, such as dark retreats, are as old as humanity, from the shamanic initiations of indigenous people to the Eleusinian mysteries of Ancient Greece.[6]

Hypnagogia

Hypnagogia is the transitional state of consciousness between wakefulness and sleep, and it is characterised by cognitive shifts whereby our subconscious becomes more suggestible, which can lead to visual, auditory or tactile hallucinations. One literature review suggested that 72–77 per cent of people experience this.[7] As a result, our dreams are often related to the last things that we saw or heard at night, which is why action boards can be most effective if viewed last thing before bed.*

Keep a dream journal by your bed and try to work out the factors during your waking life that may be impacting your dreams, or what signs are being sent to you in your dreams.

Going on a week-long dark retreat is not going to be practical for most people, but the good news is that, with advances in cognitive sciences, we now have a much deeper understanding of how to induce similar states physiologically. This includes elevating neurotransmitters by dancing to your favourite music,

---

* I wrote about this in more detail in *The Source*.

increasing heart rate variability (the miniscule variations in intervals between heartbeats that are used as an indicator of health, with high heart rate variability being associated with the parasympathetic state and the good emotional regulation associated with it) through meditation and breathwork, and changing brainwave states via polyrhythmic music, somatic work, breathwork, light, electrical or magnetic stimulation, and psychedelics.[8] I will describe some of these techniques in more detail in Part 2.

Studies have also shown that it is possible to gain many of the benefits of an NDE simply by learning about them in more detail. In his book, Dr Greyson cites one study involving students at Miami University in Ohio,[9] one at Montana State University,[10] two at the University of Connecticut[11] and another at Massey University in New Zealand[12] that reported the following benefits from learning about NDEs in various academic settings, including sociology, nursing and psychology classes:

- greater concern for and compassion for others

- greater self-worth

- less fear of dying

- greater appreciation for life

- better self-acceptance

- enhanced feelings of spirituality

- less interest in material possessions and personal achievement

Interestingly, the Miami University students even reported feeling the benefits of learning about NDEs up to a year later.

Believing in signs and using them in my life give me many of the same benefits that someone would get from an NDE or a dark retreat, but in a much more accessible way. For instance, if you have an NDE, and you believe that there's a beautiful afterlife, that you can come back or that your loved ones are still there, then you don't feel that same sense of loss. And if you believe that signs are from your lost loved one, although they're no longer in the physical world, you can still feel connected to them. This can make you feel less afraid of death and more confident in life, as well as all the other benefits that Dr Greyson has seen in his studies. Signs can increase your overall appreciation of life and promote feelings of joy, awe and wonder, which can lead to a whole new perspective on life, too. This is why I believe signs to be such a beneficial and remarkable addition to the human experience.

My friend Sabrina Percy, who has a master's in psychology with a specialisation in business, summed it up nicely:

> If a person thinks that when a loved one dies, that's it, they've completely gone, it could make them feel less hopeful and more alone in the world. But if they choose to believe that little signs are their loved one's way of telling them that they're still there in some way, looking out for them, they could feel loved, guided and protected. We can see how that would have a radical difference in someone's well-being and outlook on life.

Once you start being guided by signs, life is never the same again. It is so much more beautiful and feels like you are dancing in tune with the universe.

The Case for Spirituality in Your Life

While the narrative in the West in particular is dominated by the need to explain things in scientific terms, today approximately 6 billion people or 85 per cent of the world population identify with a religion, demonstrating that spiritual belief in the separation of the mind and body is still an important concept in most people's lives.[13] And when I say spirituality, I do not necessarily mean organised religion. You can feel a spiritual connection by appreciating the beauty and grandeur of nature, for example. This is one of the reasons why I believe that we should be a little less quick to dismiss it and more open to what spirituality has to offer; it is clearly something that human beings are drawn to and need.

We connect with nature, creativity and spirituality because they have much to teach us. As such, the things we need to be happy and healthy and to thrive today have been staring us in the face for millennia. We don't need to learn so much as *remember*.

Science has replaced spirituality as the predominant way in which we assign meaning to and understand the world, but we still need spirituality for solace and a comforting view of life and death. Our ancestors were more in tune with the continuous cycle of nature, and their belief that the spirit or consciousness continues to exist is tied up in this knowledge of continual regeneration. Many of us don't necessarily believe in life after death because we can't prove it. But ancient peoples didn't need to prove it – they saw it in nature. Understanding the cycle of nature leads to an understanding that you're part of something much bigger than yourself, and that there are powers outside your control. Nothing in nature disappears – there's a continual process of recycling, and of energy and matter being repurposed. (We'll look at reconnecting with nature in order to bring the transformative benefits of signs into our lives in Chapter 7.)

I believe that signs are a bit like a universal language that is shared by all people, past and present. This makes me feel connected to something bigger than myself, with a more holistic outlook, which seems especially important at a time when people seem more fragmented and isolated than ever before. The need for spirituality, which is seen across all cultures and goes back to ancient times and beyond, offers a point of commonality and a greater sense of purpose. If you see everything through a scientific lens, you are not experiencing all that life has to offer. I always say that connection to self, connection to others and caring for our environment are the three pillars of a spiritual and therefore purposeful life. However, as I mentioned previously, many of us have lost sight of spirituality in our lives, so signs can help us to regain trust in ourselves, each other and the universe on a daily basis.

We have evolved to be spiritual beings, and there is a psychological need that is being denied if we allow our rationality to close off the possibility that we can use signs to help guide us, comfort us and bring us joy. If your first reaction is to question whether those signs are true, you may be asking the wrong thing – you have been primed by our rational age to always look for the evidence, but how is this serving you?

I used to see signs before I thought they were from lost loved ones, and they had value in my life. Once you start living like this, it is very clear when something is actually a sign and when it's not, because it feels different. It's kind of awe-inspiring when it's a sign, and it feels a bit weak and like you're trying to make it happen when it's not something worth paying attention to. However, getting to this point is a learning process and doesn't just happen overnight – you need to practise and, in time, you will become more fluent, like learning a new language. This means that there may be something of a leap of faith to begin with when you are not so attuned to signs, but once you begin to reap the rewards, you will be more inclined to trust your signs more, and they will come to you more easily.

Even if you are not fully convinced that signs are from beyond, that's okay. You can still benefit from bringing signs into your life. If nothing else, you have much to gain from raising your awareness and noticing things that you might otherwise have missed. And if signs are not in fact from beyond but instead provide us with meaning or guidance thanks to the connections we make in our own minds, that still tells us something about what's important to us right now. Knowing where a sign comes from is less vital than what it can do for you, whether that is providing you with comfort and solace or guidance and inspiration, all of which will lead to a greater sense of purpose in life.

On her podcast *The Telepathy Tapes*, Ky Dickens challenges the notion propounded by materialism that only things that can be observed and measured can be proven. And while this might be true, it doesn't address the question of whether or not things that are beyond observation and measurement can have value. Why shouldn't we go with things that we feel and experience even if they can't be observed or measured? If we can learn to trust ourselves and our instincts and hone our intuition, how much more value could we receive from life? It is simply not true that just because something can't be proven (currently) it has no value. What might happen if you listened to your gut instinct next time?

How to Recognise Signs

So, what are signs and how do you include them in your daily life? There are no hard-and-fast rules when it comes to what constitutes a sign, and your own frame of reference and interpretation are key, but there are some signs that seem to be common to many people; for example, many signs seem to come from nature in the shape of white feathers in unexpected places, animals and birds (like robins), and butterflies. A lot of people also see signs in shapes in unexpected places. For instance, I take note of when I see a heart in an unusual context, such as a heart shape in a paving stone or a vegetable shaped like one. Music and song lyrics are also commonly thought to be signs.

However, some of the most widespread signs that people see are numbers. For example, the number 11 or the time 11.11 and other repeated numbers are considered by some people to be spiritually significant and are sometimes described as 'angel numbers', which convey a sign from the universe, a lost loved one or a guardian angel. The number 11 is also symbolic of the spiritual notion of twin flames. You are probably more familiar with the idea of soulmates, two souls who are drawn together, often romantically, and who usually have lessons to learn from one another. A twin flame, on the other hand, is when a soul grew so full of love that it split and two people carry half each. When you meet your twin flame, there's a sense that you have known one another for ever and that you belong together (similar to the concept of soul families mentioned earlier).

I also see 44 a lot, which is said to be a message from your angels that you are being guided and supported; 11 and 44 are part of my connection with Robin. Different numbers may hold special meaning to you.

You can consult numerology to find out the accepted meaning of numbers, but I think it is ultimately more impactful if you can identify numbers that are meaningful to you, just as other types of signs are ultimately personal and unique to each individual and who they are maintaining their connection with.

Knowing and asking for your signs

Use your journal to help you work out what your signs are. Jot down any repeating numbers, synchronicities, symbols or animals that grab your attention, and ask yourself what sort of shapes or objects have always fascinated you. For me, it was hearts and stars to begin with and then later the infinity symbol. Now, white feathers and robins have special meaning for me, too.

I also think it is worth setting rules around the validity of your signs – you have to be able to determine what is and isn't a sign, otherwise everything could be one. Sometimes once isn't enough and I have to see the same sign three times; some people say a sign has to occur when something appears when you go out of your way – taking a different route home, for example.

Once you've worked out what your signs are, ask for them when you need them and write what you've asked for and why into your journal, then wait for the unmistakeable sign to appear! By the time you finish this book, I would love you to be confident that you can ask for a specific sign so that when it comes to you, you know you are on the right path. Don't lose heart if it takes a while for your signs to come to you – as I mentioned above, it takes some practice and might not happen for you straightaway. I feel confident, however, that you will be able to access your signs when you really need them. The subsequent chapters are also intended to help you bring signs into your life more easily, so you can return to your journal later once you have made some of the other changes in your life that I recommend.

How to ask for a sign

1. Meditate, take a long, relaxing bath or go for a walk in nature to put yourself in the best condition to ask for a specific sign.

2. Think of something you need guidance or help with. Or just think about someone from beyond who you would love a sign from.

3. Be very specific about what that sign should be, and make it very personal to you and that person; for example, an in-joke or special memory.

4. Send them love and gratitude and ask to see the sign, perhaps in a particular environment and by a certain time.

5. Sometimes when I feel I need more reassurance, I ask to see the same sign three times in a short window of time so I can't dismiss it as a coincidence.

6. When you receive the sign or signs, note them in your journal.

7. If you feel comfortable doing so, share what you have found with your friends so that you can help others to find signs too.

I believe that magnetic desire – tapping into strong emotions such as love and joy, or fear and sadness – is sometimes necessary to call in a sign. On the day of a recent supermoon, I was feeling really distressed, and I said to Robin, 'If I don't get a sign from you, I don't know if I can carry on.' I immediately had a strong feeling that I was somehow going to see him 'with the moon'. Later that evening, I went up to the roof terrace, but the moon was obscured by some nearby tower blocks. Even though I thought it might take a couple hours for it to become visible, half an hour later I felt compelled to go back up to the roof. When I got there, the moon was high in the sky, and the jet streams of two aeroplanes had crossed nearby. I took a photo of it and sent it to a friend and said, 'Look, Robin sent me a kiss.' She quickly replied and said, 'Oh my goodness, can you see the cloud that looks like the profile of someone who's blowing the kiss?' It was just like a photo of Robin from our wedding. Some people might say, 'You're looking at a cloud and making it what you want it to be to make you feel better', but I think it's more than that. If you're willing to open your mind to the possibility that magnetic desire propels a form of communication that we cannot yet explain, your experience of life will be that much richer.

What happened during the supermoon coincided with me realising that signs weren't just a way of dealing with Robin's death, which was in the past, but could also help me as I moved forward. At hard times, whether that was just to do with grief or whether it was because something else was going on, I started to feel like he was helping me and protecting me. There is comfort on the one hand and guidance on the other. Grief is hard enough to navigate, but it often comes with practical ramifications about how you live. Comfort is for grief or when times are hard, and guidance is for showing you how to overcome struggles and challenges.

Now, when I am staring down a big decision, I feel bolstered with the knowledge that I have access to someone or something that knows a lot more than I do. It's always beneficial to acknowledge what you don't know.

It reminds me of what Dr Greyson was saying. There is a bigger reality that we can access, in the same way that our brains might be able to access a larger source of consciousness if we were to remove some of the filters. The algorithms of streaming services offer a useful analogy. If you watch a lot of romcoms, the algorithm will think that's all you're interested in and show you more of the same. However, if you watch a wider, more eclectic range of films, the algorithm will reveal more of what is available. If we rely solely on ourselves or on the people around us – although both are valuable – we narrow our perspective, and we might miss solutions and support. Accessing signs is a way of widening the resources available to us.

But we also need to create the right conditions in ourselves to see signs. We've seen that our ability to see signs is an extension of our intuitive abilities, so we need to put ourselves in the best position for these to excel – if you are closed-minded and distracted, you'll never see them. The next part of the book looks at how you can create the right conditions for your signs to appear.

KEY TAKEAWAYS

1. Signs can give you purpose in life.
2. Signs can change the way you live your life – with trust and guidance instead of worry and doubt.
3. Creativity, nature, spirituality, movement and breathwork are some of the ways to expand your consciousness and bring signs into your life.

PART

OPENING
YOUR
MIND TO
SIGNS

TWO

For as long as I can remember, I have been a spiritual person, and I have always felt like an old soul, someone who has been here before a few times – you know? When I was 15, my grandma, Joan, died. It was a huge loss to my small family. I'd spent a lot of time with her growing up and we had a lovely relationship. She taught me how to knit and cook, and I have many fond memories of the jam tarts we used to make together!

After she passed, I never felt like she was far away. I'd often ask her to ward off bad spirits when I sensed them, and then would feel almost immediate relief and peacefulness. In the years that passed, as I grew into adulthood, I started receiving visits from robins. Now, I'm not talking about every robin I see, but specific visits strike a chord. Sometimes they would be in my garden for a while, other times they'd fly close to me and land on a branch nearby and just look at me. Just last month one came and sat on the table I was at with my dog. It is inexplicable as to why, but I have felt these robins are my grandma sending me a message. The visits have often been at times I've struggled with my mental health and they have brought comfort; when I'm at a crossroads and pondering what to do, and they have brought me clarity; or right at a big change in my life, just to let me know she is there beside me. One day, I told my mum about this and she cried – she told me she had also been receiving visits from robins for years since Joan passed and had also felt it was her; it's now something we share. I know Joan is guiding me, giving me little supportive nudges when I need it, and it's a special feeling.

– *Mimi*

We have already raised awareness of signs to some extent in Part 1, but there is much more we can do to make ourselves receptive to receiving them. If we are too stressed or busy to pause and notice what is around us, we are unlikely to see the signs that I believe can guide us to a fuller and more joyful life.

In the chapters that follow, I will explain some of the key things you can do to prime yourself to take advantage of this wonderful resource. This starts with tuning in to your senses to raise awareness of yourself and the world at large, followed by gaining a better understanding and use of your intuition. I then go on to describe how you can create the conditions to receive and interpret signs by introducing simple practices into your life to reconnect with creativity, nature and other people.

These practices have health and well-being benefits in and of themselves, which I will share with you, but the process of learning new skills and accessing previously untapped aspects of your mental faculties has a transformative effect on your brain more generally as a result of neuroplasticity – the brain's amazing capacity for growth and development. It was once thought that the brain remained static once we reached adulthood, but we now know that it is, in fact, able to form new neural pathways at any age, opening up the reality that our thought patterns and behaviours are not fixed and we therefore have the power to change them – and probably more so than we are even aware of today.

The four steps of behaviour change underpinned by neuroplasticity are raised awareness, focused attention, deliberate practice and accountability, and they are intrinsic to the advice and exercises that I describe in Part 2. This is not as daunting as it may sound. It's really about achieving incremental progress by introducing micro-habits in our everyday lives that are easy and enjoyable but, taken as a whole, have a real impact on our brains. My motto is: 'Change ten things by 1 per cent rather than one thing by 10 per cent.' A good analogy for this is when I wanted to incorporate daily yoga practice into my routine and said to my yoga teacher that I was finding it hard to fit in a 90-minute class or do 45–60 minutes at home every single day. Her response was that even if I just lay on my yoga mat for five minutes, that constituted daily practice. So, I now go to a class when I can and do half an hour or more at home if I have time; otherwise, I lie on my mat for five minutes or do a couple of simple poses, and that's enough.

The same goes for everything I am suggesting in this book. If you do lots of smaller things when you can, you can build up to the bigger things, and this will have a positive impact on your physical and mental well-being, but it will also provide you with the psychological safety to take healthy risks, think more flexibly and heighten your awareness of the potential available to all of us if we look for it.

If you believe in the possibility of esoteric signs, this section of the book shows you how you can help yourself see them. But if you still need a little convincing, you can benefit from unshackling yourself from the stress of modern life, being more consciously aware of your surroundings and listening to your intuition.

CHAPTER 4

CONNECT WITH YOUR SENSES

I n the early days after Robin died, I would wake up absolutely freezing cold and have to blast the heating up so high that by the time visitors arrived after lunchtime, the house was like a sauna and I had to open the windows to let in some cool air. At first, I thought my brain was playing tricks on me; it took me several days to realise that Robin was in the morgue, probably in a refrigerated drawer. It was then that it occurred to me that we could still be connected somehow, with my senses emulating my perception of his situation and manifesting in my own body through my sense of temperature. This was particularly significant to me because he hated feeling cold. That it was my sense of temperature that was triggered at this time was an early indication to me that our senses are more important than we realise and that having a better understanding of them might help to unlock signs we might otherwise be missing in our lives. I didn't really understand what this meant at the time, and I can't know if that connection I felt was real or psychological, but with all that I have now learnt about our amazing senses, I am open to that possibility. At the very least, I can see that my brain was embodying what I was feeling emotionally but was not able to articulate consciously.

Whenever I ask any of my friends or clients, 'How many senses do we have?' they invariably say five. Occasionally, someone will say something like, 'Isn't there supposed to be a sixth sense?' Even then, there isn't any agreement about what that sixth one might be. Some say balance and others intuition. But, for the most part, it's sight, smell, sound, taste and touch that they mention. And it's not really surprising, as this is what most of us are taught from a young age.

In actual fact, scientists have discovered that most of us have 34 senses (more on these in just a bit). Furthermore, the science of our senses keeps evolving. It is important that we understand this complexity, because our senses are the best tools at our disposal for tuning in to the here and now, quietening the noise and distraction of modern life and understanding what our bodies are telling us.

In this chapter, I will explain how you perceive the world and how you can move beyond your everyday awareness, not only to ensure you spot the signs that are presented to you, but also to harness a range of other health benefits. I believe that we may not yet understand the full depth of our abilities, and tuning in to the senses we understand is the first step towards exploring that.

The Complexity of Our Senses

Before we look at how to tune in to our senses more effectively, it is first helpful to understand just how complex they are, and to acknowledge those senses that we might not even be aware of. And that starts with understanding what a sense actually is. From a medical, physiological point of view, a sense is the faculty by which the body perceives a stimulus. A receptor in our bodies is activated by that stimulus and sends a signal to our brain so that it can generate an appropriate response. For example, receptors for smell are located in the olfactory epithelium, which lines the roof of your nasal cavity. When particles of odour bind to that receptor, it creates a process that carries information to the brain that leads to a reaction, such as wrinkling your nose in disgust at a bad smell or inhaling more deeply to enhance the pleasure you get from the scent of flowers. Similarly, the organ of Corti in the cochlea of the inner ear contains hair cells that are the primary audio receptors. When these are stimulated, that is the first step in the process of how we decode music, language, nature sounds and all of the other noises around us.

The senses can be broadly differentiated by those that are activated by stimuli from outside the body (known as exteroception) and those from within (interoception). Exteroception is the perception of the external world through our senses, and it is a critical process that allows us to adapt to our environment. Interoception, on the other hand, is an umbrella term for the wide range of internal senses that send signals to our brains about the workings of our bodies, because lots of things are constantly being activated internally that we're not aware of.

The 34 senses at our disposal[1]

Common name	Technical name (where applicable)
1. Sight	Photoreception
2. Light detection (passing of time)	Chronoception
3. Hearing	Auditory perception
4. Smell	Olfaction
Taste	Gustation
5. Salty taste	
6. Sweet taste	
7. Bitter taste	
8. Sour taste	
9. Umami taste	
Touch	Somatosensory/tactile
10. Pressure touch	
11. Vibration touch	

12. Gentle, slow-moving contact touch	
13. Itch touch	Pruritus
Pain	**Nociception**
14. Pain caused by extreme heat or cold	
15. Pain caused by dangerous chemicals	
16. Pain caused by physical damage	
Temperature	**Thermoception**
17. Cool temperature	
18. Warm temperature	
Movement sense	**Proprioception**
19. Body mapping/joint position sense	
20. Sense of effort, force and heaviness	
Balance	**Equilibrioception**
21. Head rotation balance	
22. Vertical motion	
23. Horizontal motion	
'Staying alive' senses	**Interoception**
24. Heartbeat	
25. Blood pressure	Baroreception
26. Carbon dioxide	
27. Oxygen	
28. Lung stretch	
29. Cerebrospinal fluid pH receptors	
30. Plasma osmotic pressure	
31. The immune system	
Appetite and waste senses	**Gastrointestinal and genitourinary systems**
32. Stomach fullness	
33. Bladder fullness	
34. Rectal fullness	

The exteroceptive senses (1–23) are the ones that we are more familiar with, including the five that we are taught about in primary school. But even these are more complex than we realise. For example, our eyes do not just facilitate sight (1), they also detect light levels (2), which is thought to have a role in our perception of time passing (also known as chronoception, which I discuss in more detail below).

Taste is a good case in point when it comes to the complexity of our senses, as it can be subdivided into the different receptors on the tongue for the five flavour profiles: salty (5), sweet (6), bitter (7), sour (8) and umami or savoury (9). The addition of umami as a distinct flavour that we are able to sense didn't happen until the mid-1980s.[2]

Like taste, touch can also be subdivided. On the one hand, we are able to detect how much pressure is being applied to our bodies or that we are applying to something else (10), but we can also sense physical vibrations (11) around us. Gentle, slow-moving contact (12) is how we sense physical touch from another person, and feeling an itch (13) is another form of touch, the medical term for which is pruritus. The exteroceptive

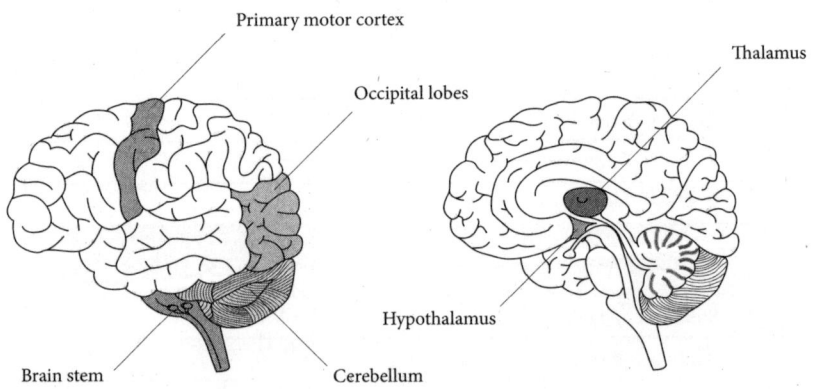

Brain regions associated with senses

senses are processed in a variety of areas throughout the brain; for example, vision is processed in the occipital lobes at the base of the skull.

Beyond the five common exteroceptive senses, there are a number of others at our disposal that help us to make sense of our place in the world but that we might not be aware of or think of as senses. For example, proprioception is the term for the senses that monitor and help us to control our bodies in our physical environments. Joint position sense or body mapping (19) is a sense of where your limbs, head and torso are in space. It is this sense that allows you to touch your nose with your eyes closed, and it relies heavily on sensory processing areas in the parietal lobe of the brain. There is also the sense of physical effort, force and heaviness (20), which has been linked to areas of the brain that contribute to the generation of movement, including the primary motor cortex, cerebellum and brain stem. Although distinct areas of the brain are primarily responsible for different proprioceptive senses, there is significant overlap in the neural pathways between these areas as they feed information to each other.

We may not be aware of them most of the time, but our proprioception senses are constantly sending our brains important messages. Say that you have tea in the same mug every morning. Over time, your body non-consciously recognises how heavy that mug is and therefore how much effort is required to lift it from the kitchen counter. If I sneaked in and replaced it with a replica that was made of polystyrene, when you picked it up, you would apply too much force and the tea would fly out of the mug. Similarly, if you pick up a fragile glass, you are able to sense how much pressure to apply without crushing it. Or, if you wanted to swat a fly, you wouldn't slam your hand so hard onto the table that you would hurt yourself.

And there is more that you probably aren't consciously aware of. Balance, or equilibrioception, can also be characterised as a sense, and it is influenced by a range of receptors in our bodies detecting three different types of movement: head rotation (21) and vertical (22) and horizontal (23) motion. Your Eustachian tubes in your ears and your cerebral spinal fluid play a part in how you detect whether you are upright or tipping, so you can correct yourself if needed. Although you might not have thought of balance as being a sense, it is an important one to be aware of, as it plays a big role in our physical well-being and how well we age (something I discuss in more detail below).

As you can see, there are a lot of external stimuli that our bodies are able to process. At the same time, there is as much if not more going on inside each of us – these are the interoceptive senses. Receptors throughout your body are constantly monitoring your heart rate (24) and blood pressure (25), how much carbon dioxide (26) and oxygen (27) are in your blood system, lung stretch (28), which determines how deeply you're breathing, cerebrospinal fluid pH levels (29), which also plays a part in the regulation of carbon dioxide and oxygen concentrations in the blood, and plasma osmotic pressure (30), which measures blood volume and salt balance. The immune system (31) is a newly discovered interoceptive sense that I'll speak about in more detail below. Appetite and waste senses, meanwhile, are more or less self-explanatory, as they prompt sensations that most of us experience quite strongly, and on a daily basis. You know when you are hungry or if you ate too much (32), and you know when you need to empty your bladder (33) or bowels (34).

Via these interoceptive senses, the body is continually sending signals to the brain about its own operation so that it can control homeostasis – that is, maintain equilibrium in your system. This is regulated in the thalamus, hypothalamus and brain stem regions of the brain.

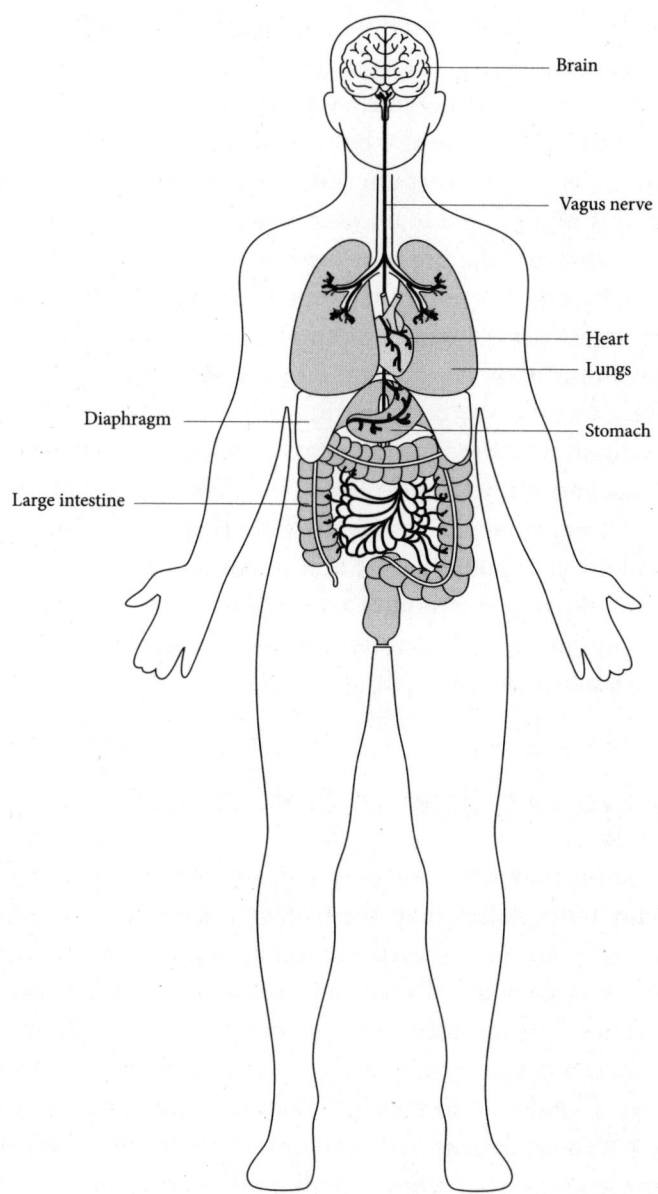

Brain

Vagus nerve

Heart

Lungs

Diaphragm

Stomach

Large intestine

The vagus nerve

The vagus nerve, a key part of the autonomic nervous system (part of the peripheral nervous system, which includes all of the nerves in our bodies apart from the brain and spinal cord, which make up the central nervous system), also plays a crucial role in maintaining homeostasis by regulating various physiological functions, including heart rate, digestion and immune responses. The vagus nerve is made up of two nerves (left and right) that run directly from the brain to your large intestine via the lungs and diaphragm. *Vagus* means 'wandering' in Latin, which is apt, as the vagus nerves are the longest in the autonomic nervous system and connect to many different body parts.

There's a two-way conversation going on between your body and brain that you're mostly not aware of, but it's happening all the time, and it's helping to keep you alive and in equilibrium. Furthermore, none of these processes happen in isolation – they all occur simultaneously and in concert with one another, thereby allowing our bodies to function with little conscious input from us. It really is a remarkable system, full of complexity and sophistication.

The Evolving Science of the Senses

Although it may have come as a surprise to you that we have so many more senses than the five we are all aware of, the list above is by no means fixed and final; our knowledge of what the body is capable of continues to evolve as we make new discoveries. For instance, only in recent years has the immune system been considered by researchers as constituting a sense.[3] It plays a vital role in keeping us healthy by detecting pathogenic micro-organisms and sending signals to the brain, which in turn sends messages to the body so that an immune response can be triggered and controlled. An example of this in practice might be the immune sensory system detecting a harmful micro-organism in the body, and the brain in response prompting sickness behaviours, such as resting alone, in order that the body can save energy and reduce the likelihood that it is exposed to any other pathogenic material. The mechanisms by which this bidirectional communication takes place are still the subject of research, but we know that immune cells can produce and receive neurotransmitters (a chemical messenger) and that the vagus nerve is also a major conduit of information transfer between the immune system and the brain.

The animal kingdom offers another good illustration of the fact that how we perceive the world is not the only way to do so. Humans and animals share many senses, but in some cases animals have developed far superior capabilities to us. A good example is the far greater sensitivity of dogs to smell. In fact, it has been shown that dogs can even smell illness and imminent death in humans.[4] There are also a number of senses that humans don't have but other animals do. For example, dolphins can communicate using echolocation, which is also known as biosonar, and some organisms exhibit magnetoreception, which is the ability to detect the earth's magnetic field. This is how some birds are able to navigate long distances.[5] These animal senses point to the fact that there are other ways of experiencing reality in nature. So, we might not be able to navigate using the earth's magnetic field, but there may be other things that we can do that we aren't aware of yet.

For example, some people believe we have a second nose that is not connected to the brain. It is called the vomeronasal, or Jacobson's, organ, and although its presence has been confirmed by anatomical studies of the nasal cavity, its potential function is much debated.[6] In dogs and other mammals, it has a role in the detection of pheromones,[7] so it is possible that future research will discover a similar role in humans, further highlighting how much we still have to learn about our senses and bodies more generally.

Some people already have heightened olfactory abilities. They are known as 'super smellers', and some can even smell certain diseases. This is known as hereditary hyperosmia, and the most well-known example is retired nurse Joy Milne, who was able to smell her husband's Parkinson's disease by detecting a change in his odour six years before he was diagnosed with the illness. This led to the charity Parkinson's UK funding research into the possibility of using what Joy had discovered to create tests to help diagnose Parkinson's earlier, even before the physical symptoms are visible,[8] and scientists at the University of Manchester have now created a skin-swab test that can detect chemical compounds unique to people with Parkinson's disease.[9] Without Joy's remarkable sense of smell, this breakthrough might never have happened.

Other people have been shown to experience their senses differently from what we might consider to be the norm; for example, the neurological phenomenon known as synaesthesia, when stimulation of one sense triggers a response in another sense. Grapheme–colour synaesthesia is where people associate certain numbers or letters with specific colours, lexical–gustatory synaesthesia is where hearing or reading words triggers a certain taste sensation and chromesthesia involves seeing colours when you hear certain sounds, including music. Although the mechanisms for synaesthesia are not yet understood, it further demonstrates that our senses are more complex than we realise and able to evolve in unexpected ways.

People with synaesthesia and Joy's heightened sense of smell are obviously outliers, but what if all of us are capable of more than we realise when it comes to our senses? What we know and accept as fact today is not necessarily what we will know to be true tomorrow, and by tuning in to our senses more deliberately, it may be that it is possible to raise our awareness of ourselves and the wider world. Our senses could also be indicators of emotional states and connections to the world around us and to others, such as my experience of feeling cold when Robin was in the morgue.

Your personal perception

The fact that there are more senses than we realise, coupled with the new discoveries that are being made all the time, shows us that our knowledge about what the senses are capable of is not fixed. At the same time, our perception of the world is also fluid and malleable. A good example of this is how we perceive time.

Our sense of time is just as complex as our senses more generally. To begin with, there is a distinction to be made between our subjective experience of time passing (chronoception) and our internal body clocks (circadian rhythm). In terms of the latter, there's a non-conscious physiological process going on whereby your body knows when to wake up, for example, and can sense the time of day with a high degree of accuracy. This circadian rhythm is thought to play out in the eyes themselves, with the difference in light levels between night and day influencing the rods and cones of the retina.[10] The process by which our environment influences our body clocks is called entrainment. This involves the daily light–dark cycle influencing our sleep–wake cycle by prompting the production of melatonin to help us fall asleep and cortisol to help us wake up. But even though we know that light plays a big part in regulating our body clocks, there is a lot more yet to discover about how this works physiologically.

Our knowledge about chronoception is also a work in progress. Although the mechanism for chronoception has not been strictly defined, and it has not been shown to be tied to any one sensory system, research has found that it takes place in the basal ganglia, deep in the base of the brain, and in the right parietal lobe located on the surface of the right side of the brain.[11]

Despite the fact that our understanding of the mechanism for chronoception is still a work in progress, what is not in question is that there is a subjective quality to the way we sense time. In fact, this is something that has been acknowledged for thousands of years, with the Ancient Greeks recognising the difference between chronological time (*chronos*) and subjective time (*kairos*). This is a good example of something people have known for millennia and yet we still don't understand how it works. When it comes to the brain and perception, there is still so much for us to learn.

Tuning in to Your Senses

The malleability of our perception means that we can raise awareness of our senses in the moment to change our view of the world and, through this, quieten and slow the distractions of modern life, opening the way for signs. If we do this regularly, these ways of relating to the world become imprinted on the brain via neuroplasticity. For example, I use essential oils in the bath and have diffusers and incense around my house. Aside from the associated health benefits of olfactory enrichment, which we'll come on to, I also believe that scents can be signs that are sent to us. For example, if I step off a plane and notice the smell of a different country, or I walk past a shop and a certain aroma wafts out, it could be a sign. This is just one example of how I purposefully engage my senses in order to enhance my ability to notice things, meaning that if a sign is sent to me, I will actually be aware of it. By raising awareness of our senses, we are less likely to be reactive to the stimuli around us, and better regulated in our nervous systems, so that we can be proactive about choosing and asking for signs, and using a whole-body approach to access our intuition and interpret the messages we are sent.

With practice, you too can train yourself to focus more on what you see, hear, smell and feel in the moment in order to quieten the noise and distraction of modern life. There are various meditations and exercises that can heighten your awareness of your senses. Below are three that I recommend for this purpose.

Taste meditation

You can do this while walking or sitting.

1. Take a raisin and slowly chew it for one minute, trying not to swallow your saliva during this time.

2. As you chew it, focus on the effect on your taste buds.

3. Visualise the vine on which the grape grew in sunny climes, and the rain on the soil that nourished the vine. Imagine the leaves and fruit growing under blue skies. See the hands that picked the grapes and laid them out in the sun to dry. Travel through time and visualise the process of boxing up the raisins and delivering them to your country, to your town, to your local shop, and you bringing them home and picking the raisin for this meditation.

4. When you have finished, swallow the raisin.

Sound meditation

1. Sit in a comfortable place and position.

2. Take three deep breaths and then breathe normally.

3. Focus on the sounds around you in general.

4. Direct your attention first to the sounds that are closest and then to those that are furthest away, followed by the sounds that are loudest and then the ones that are quietest.

5. Slowly bring your attention inwards and notice that although there are sounds outside, there is quietness and stillness inside.

6. Over time, prioritise the internal sense of calmness that resides within you.

Visual exercise

1. Go outside or look out of a window.

2. Focus on something small and close up in detail, such as a leaf or the palm of your hand, for one minute.

3. Afterwards, focus on something large and in the distance, such as a tree or a building, for one minute.

4. Repeat this exercise regularly until you feel that you can slow down and more easily notice what is around you in the moment.

These exercises are about focusing your attention on the moment, but some interesting insights might also surface while you're doing them, so it is worth reflecting on what came up for you and journalling about it afterwards. This means you can reap the benefit of being in the moment, and also take away any lessons that will help you moving forward. Over time and with repetition, you will be able to tune in to your senses effortlessly in the moment, and this will help you to notice signs more easily, too.

Reducing Stress

Stress – a state that's so commonplace today and associated with that feeling we discussed in the Introduction of life passing by at 100 miles per hour – is a key factor in us not being able to access our signs, because it narrows our awareness and clouds our intuition. In the next chapter, I discuss how to harness intuition in more depth, but first it is helpful to become more aware of indicators of stress and understand how to overcome them.

Your heart beating more quickly and your breath becoming shallower may be appropriate responses if you are in a life-or-death situation, but they are less helpful if you're in an everyday one, such as at work, which is why you need to be able to regulate your stress levels in the moment. The good news is that those physiological responses are messages from your body that can help you to intervene and mitigate the impact of the stress you are feeling. The senses that fall under the bracket of interoception can be both conscious and non-conscious – for example, we are usually not aware of our heartbeat, but if we turn our attention to it, we can get a sense of how slow or fast it is beating. Things like the detection of oxygen or carbon dioxide levels in the blood, on the other hand, are always non-conscious processes. But even though you don't necessarily have conscious access to these senses, you can have an impact on them by changing your breathing rate.

The key is to recognise the signals your body is sending you as soon as possible, giving you the time to act upon them, especially if they are warning you that something is amiss. For example, usually you breathe without thinking about it, but you can intervene and consciously decide how fast or slow, or deep or shallow, each breath is. This is important, because when people are stressed, they tend to breathe more shallowly or even hold their breath for periods of time.

Neglecting chronic stress or moments of debilitating acute stress not only has obvious health-related implications, but also means that you will be less open to receiving messages from your intuition or receiving signs, since you are already missing interoceptive signals from your body and your awareness of yourself and the world is not allowing you to live life to the full.

But why do people breathe less when they're stressed? You would think that the body would want to take on more oxygen, rather than restricting something that is so vital. One theory is that it goes back to early humans running away from predators on the savannah.[12] When you're running, your breathing rate goes up and becomes shallower, allowing your body to take on more oxygen quickly, although this can also lead to an imbalance in the gases in our blood and can cause palpitations or even fainting. We are still programmed to do that same thing, even though the opposite reaction of breathing more deeply and slowly would seem more appropriate. It's physiological – our brain tells us to breathe in a certain way, even though we're not actually performing the physical action that was prompted by it in the past via hormones and neurotransmitters being triggered by a perceived threat. It's a very primal response. I don't like to use the word 'hard-wired', as it doesn't account for the neuroplastic quality of the brain to grow and change throughout life, but it is fair to say that it is soft-wired in there and takes conscious effort to override.

If you're stressed and in the sympathetic state (known as 'fright, fight and flight'), you're less likely to notice signs, because it's taking all of your energy just to get by. That's why you need to strive towards having a regulated nervous system and being in the parasympathetic state (sometimes referred to as 'rest and digest' and associated with feeling relaxed) by managing your stress levels. If your physical and mental resources are being used up trying to deal with chronic stress, then you're not going to have the spare bandwidth to be able to notice signs. I call it 'low-power mode' when you're dealing with stress, whereby you have less access to the executive functions of the brain, such as regulating your emotions, thinking flexibly, solving complex problems, thinking creatively and so on. Accessing signs can also be thought of as an executive function, or even a step beyond what we consider our more established executive functions to be, because I believe our brains are capable of so much more than we realise.

Vagus nerve activation

The ultimate aim of raising awareness and making the nonconscious become conscious is to promote physiological balance or homeostasis, because having your system in equilibrium reduces stress and improves emotional regulation, increasing the amount of time that you're in the parasympathetic state rather than the sympathetic state. A good way to combat stress is learning how to activate your vagus nerve, as it is also the main nerve of the parasympathetic system and helps to calm down the body after a stressful situation, promoting relaxation, digestion and rest. There are now health tech devices that can activate your vagus nerve, but there are also exercises that are easy and free that you can do yourself.

Below are three exercises that are good for lowering stress, which is an important factor in creating the right conditions to notice signs.

The mindful sigh

The 'mindful sigh' is a great exercise to do whenever you notice stress signs such as shallow breathing, increased heart rate or tension in your neck or shoulders. I often do it when I'm sitting at my desk, but any comfortable sitting position will work.

1. Inhale deeply through your nose and hold for five seconds.

2. Before exhaling, take another one-second inhale and hold for a further three seconds.

3. Exhale slowly through your mouth, as though you are sighing, for six seconds.

4. Repeat a further two times.

The purpose of the second inhale (Step 2) is to reinflate the air sacs in the lungs that collapsed when you finished your first inhale. This increases the surface area of your lungs, which allows your body to flush out the carbon dioxide more efficiently, which in turn helps you to relax, as increased carbon dioxide levels can lead to feelings of worry or anxiety and elevate blood pressure and heart rate in humans, and induce fear in animals.[13] Meanwhile, the long, sigh-like exhale signals to the brain to slow down your pulse by slightly increasing pressure in receptors located in the heart.

The half-salamander

This is another great exercise to do quickly when in a seated position, although you can also stand. It is named after the animal, as you have to mimic the way the neckless salamander moves it eyes without moving its head.

1. Relax your body and face forward.

2. Without moving your head, look as far up towards the right as you can and breathe in.

3. Keep your eyes fixed as far to the right as possible and move your right ear towards your right shoulder (you are tilting your head to the right rather than rotating it) and breathe out – hold this position until you naturally swallow or need to breathe in.

4. Return your head to its natural position and look straight ahead again and breathe out.

5. Repeat this process on the left-hand side.

The purpose of this exercise is to stimulate the vagus nerve. Because it runs through part of the diaphragm, which is our main respiratory muscle, any movement of the diaphragm stimulates the nerve, which in turn stimulates a parasympathetic, or rest-and-digest, response.

The full salamander

You need more space for this exercise, so it is one that you can build into your routine at home, rather than as a response to stress indicators while you are on the move.

1. Kneel down on all fours, keeping your back and head in a straight line, and look at the floor.

2. Without moving your head or body, look as far up to the right as you can and breathe in.

3. As in the half-salamander, tilt your head to the right by moving your right ear towards your right shoulder and

breathe out – your head should only move horizontally, not vertically.

4. At the same time, allow your spine to curve towards the right and hold this position for 30 seconds to a minute, inhaling and exhaling regularly.

5. Bring your head and spine back to a central position and move your gaze back towards the floor.

6. Repeat the process on the left-hand side.

This exercise also stimulates the vagus nerve but has a greater impact than the half-salamander, as you are using more of your body.

Enriching Your Sense of Smell

Smell is a sense that can immediately bring us into the here and now, and it can have a powerful effect on our mindset. As we've seen, our sense of smell is regulated by tissue inside the nose called the olfactory epithelium, which sends signals via the olfactory nerve to the olfactory bulb. This sits directly behind the nose in the brain, close to the limbic system, which includes the amygdala, where most of our emotions are processed, and the hippocampus, where most of our memories are formed, particularly long-term memories. When you smell something, these areas of the brain are stimulated as well, leading to the release of neurotransmitters such as dopamine, noradrenaline and serotonin, depending on the perceived smell and its associated memory or emotional context. In this way, the smell acts as a stimulus that initiates a cascade of neural activity, impacting neurotransmitter release and influencing mood and behaviour. This is why scents can trigger strong emotions and memories that go back further than those triggered by any other senses. Interestingly, smell is also the only sense that is fully developed in the womb, remaining the most developed sense until about the age of ten, and it's thought to be the only exteroceptive sense that is active even when we are asleep or in a coma.[14]

Olfactory enrichment – that is, deliberately stimulating your sense of smell – has real health benefits. For instance, it has been found that the more scents you smell on a daily basis, the better you'll likely age in terms of memory and cognition. One study showed that even minimal olfactory enrichment overnight produces improvements in cognitive and neural function in older adults by up to 226 per cent – imagine what you could do with that![15] A variety of novel smells helps to better stimulate neurons in the olfactory bulb, which in turn helps to stimulate neurons in the amygdala and hippocampus regions of the brain and the release of the neurotransmitters mentioned above.

Introducing essential oils into your environment, as I do, is one easy way you can stimulate your sense of smell in a productive way, although it is better if you can select high-quality ones to interact with the brain–body system. Products require different concentrations depending on what they are – whether it is a shower gel, bath salt, home diffuser or roll-on body product – and reputable brands adhere to these requirements. In terms of which scents to select, rose essential oil is a good one for optimism, as it promotes the release of serotonin, a neurotransmitter renowned for its happiness-inducing effects. Serotonin is also released during moments of daydreaming or mindfulness, creating feelings of tranquillity and joy. I'd also recommend bergamot essential oil, as it stimulates the release of endorphins, the brain's feel-good chemicals. These neurotransmitters induce brain states that create the best physical conditions for you to notice signs more effectively.

But even if you don't have access to essential oils, there are other simple ways of introducing olfactory enrichment into your routine:

- light a scented candle
- burn incense
- smell different flowers in a park or in your garden
- zest a lemon
- savour your morning coffee
- notice the smell of your bath and shower products
- use a pillow spray overnight
- enjoy cooking or baking aromas

By doing so, you're enriching your relationship with your environment and, through repeated stimulation, broadening your sense of smell overall. This points to the importance of positively stimulating your senses, as this plays a key role in inducing neuroplasticity growth and changes in the brain. This improved brain power can be used to improve your health, regulate your emotions better, access your intuition, improve your relationship with yourself and others, and pursue your purpose.

Slowing Down Time

Recalibrating your perception of time is another example of raising awareness of a sense and thereby taking more control of it. Because chronoception is subjective, we can slow down or speed up our sense of how much time has passed, and in this way have a direct influence on it. That is not to say that we can impact how much time has actually elapsed, but our perception means that we can feel like it's going slower or faster at times. During moments of monotony, time feels like it goes much more slowly, whereas if we have lots of points of novelty, time feels like it goes faster.

I often hear people say things like, 'It feels like you were away for ages,' or, 'I feel like my holiday was over in a flash.' The circumstances change the sense of time passing. When I travelled a lot on business, if Robin couldn't come with me, he said that the time apart in our home with me not there felt like an eternity for him, whereas I was trying to cram as much into the shortest trip possible so I could get home sooner, and was very busy and in a completely different environment, so it felt like it went quicker for me. It was a different experience for both of us due to the environmental cues over exactly the same period of time.

Many of us are time-poor, and this often leads to stress. Other people worry that they will run out of time before they get to do all the things that they want to. Slowing down our perception of how much time is passing could therefore help to empower us and is another way in which we can lower our stress levels. If you feel that you have more control over your subjective perception of time, then you can use that to your benefit by feeling like time isn't rushing away from you so much. Being more present helps you to regulate your nervous system, which contributes to lower stress, allowing you to access signs more easily.

There is an element of choice in feeling like your holiday went by in a flash – living more in the moment, for instance, will help you to think less about the passing of time. In this way, you can remove the stress of any negative ideas you have about the passing of time by being more present. The following techniques will help you to shift your perception of time.

Shifting your perception of time

- Journalling helps you to be more present, savour the events that occur in your life and realise how much you have achieved. Note down when you feel like life is whizzing by or when you feel like you've stagnated and try to work out the factors that get you into or out of a slump.

- Gratitude practices, such as naming ten things you are grateful for (see box below) or sharing with someone how much you appreciate something they've done for you, also keep you much more present and aware.

- Paying attention and noticing small details, such as wonderful little elements of nature like birdsong or spring blossoms, also promotes oxytocin release and leads to you feeling more in tune with the passing of time and the cycles of nature, which makes you realise that you are part of something much bigger. This sense of perspective helps you to slow down and prioritise what is important.

- Meditations such as the sensory ones in this chapter (see page 89) also bring a feeling of pause and a sense of time slowing down.

To reiterate, I'm not saying that you can literally change chronological time – the second hand is going to go round at the same rate regardless. What I really want to do is help you to either break out of your monotony or alleviate your stress. It's about quality time as well. You need to prioritise what's actually important to you.

The power of gratitude

Being grateful might seem pretty inconsequential in the grand scheme of things, but gratitude is actually central to our well-being. The oxytocin boost provided by gratitude leads to feelings of joy and trust (the feel-good state) that reduce the rushed feeling of stress that is caused by cortisol. I've been doing a gratitude practice for years, and if I'm stressed or in a negative mindset, it's the quickest way to bring myself out of it. When you're in a downward spiral, it can be difficult to remember this, so I have tried to train myself to remember this more quickly.

One of the best and easiest ways to start a gratitude practice is to write in your journal ten things that you're grateful for. Later, when you get more adept at it, you can just do this in your mind as soon as you feel like you need an oxytocin boost. I think ten is a good number, as the first five usually come quite easily, so going a bit further forces you to think about things to be grateful for that you might not generally acknowledge and brings about more variety.

A big game-changer for me was when I realised I was focusing my gratitude on mainly external things. Instead, I began to give thanks for internal, personal qualities, such as my resilience and creativity, which really reinforced for me that I have all of the skills needed to deal with life's challenges. If you concentrate on mainly external things, which is a natural inclination, it can actually be quite disempowering, because it makes you feel like you're reliant on those things that you can't control.

Improving Your Sense of Balance

When I had a lot of people come to visit me on a daily basis for months after Robin passed away, I noticed how many of them had to sit down or lean against a wall to put their shoes on or take them off. Age was clearly a factor, but there were also exceptions, people who were older but very physically fit or more flexible. I remember thinking, 'I'm going to make myself keep putting my shoes on standing up without holding on to anything because that's a marker of good ageing.' In the Blue Zones in places such as Sardinia or Japan, where the greatest concentration of centenarians are to be found, people who climb steep hills or squat on the floor have stronger leg muscles and are less likely to suffer from falls – one of the leading causes of death and disease in the elderly.[16]

If you're ageing well physically, you are more likely to be ageing well mentally. And being physically fitter, stronger and more resilient makes you more independent, resourceful and optimistic. As I've said, everything stems from your physical body: your mental faculties, your emotional regulation, your spiritual connection. None of those can function if the body isn't in physically good shape. You therefore have to create the physical conditions for success. If you work to improve your sense of balance by doing a simple exercise like the one below, you demonstrate to yourself in a tangible way how you can work on and better tune in to a sense. This has an impact on your ability and willingness to tune in to your other senses as a result of promoting neuroplasticity changes in the brain. This in turn can bolster your sense of trust that you can open your mind to be more aware generally and therefore enhance your ability to notice signs.

Balance exercise

The simplest exercise you can do to tune in to your sense of balance is to close your eyes and stand on one leg for as long as you can.

1. Find a flat, open space where there is nothing to hurt you if you should stumble or fall. If you feel particularly unsure of your balance, you can stand near a wall or a chair to catch yourself if necessary, or have someone around to support you.

2. Stand upright with your feet slightly apart.

3. Place your hands by your side or together in a praying position in front of your chest.

4. Lift your left foot off the ground, bend your knee and find your balance.

5. Close your eyes and try to hold the pose for as long as possible.

6. Repeat on the other side.

You will probably feel quite wobbly to begin with, but if you do it every day, you will soon notice that you feel more stable and are able to hold your balance for much longer.

We often take our bodies for granted, and it is easy to lose sight of just how remarkable they are. This is aptly demonstrated by the fact that our sensory systems are much more complex than we realise. By acknowledging this fact, not only do we open our minds to what else we might be capable of, we also increase our ability to notice and take advantage of signs.

Tuning in to your eyes, ears and every other sense at your disposal is going to be beneficial in helping you to expand your awareness of the world and your place in it. Furthermore, if you're more in touch with your senses and therefore your body, you're more likely to be able to have good physical and mental health, and you will be better able to quieten the noise and stress of everyday life, allowing you to create the right conditions to focus on what is important. This is the foundation for you being able to access your intuition and more effectively interpret the signs that you receive, which I talk about in the next chapter. It all starts with the physical and embracing the fact that you are a sensory being equipped to receive and interpret signs of all kinds.

KEY TAKEAWAYS

1. A well-regulated nervous system is key to bringing signs into your life.
2. We can enrich and hone our senses to improve cognitive and physical functions as we age.
3. We are capable of so much more than we realise, and tuning in to our senses is the first step in us being able to notice our signs.

CHAPTER 5

CONNECT WITH YOUR INTUITION

created one of the most significant action boards of my life in December 2015 when I saw an advert in a magazine that read 'Joy comes out of the blue'. I don't normally include words on my boards, but I felt drawn to this phrase. In early February 2016, I met Robin for the first time on a flight. Then, in late February, I wrote in my journal that if I saw three infinity symbols, it would mean the person I was going to marry was already in my life. I didn't for one moment think that person would be Robin, because we didn't start dating until three months later. It was only when we were in a relationship that I looked back and connected the dots. I'd chosen infinity signs because I'd noticed the Virgin logo, which is a kind of asymmetric infinity sign, on adverts all over the place. Soon, I saw my first one – an elastic band in the shape of a figure of eight on the pavement, and then I flew to Istanbul to speak at a conference, and another speaker had a wedding ring with the infinity symbol engraved on it, which was so small I almost missed it. Not long afterwards, I was on the Tube, sitting down, and there was a girl standing in front of me who had a small gap between her trainers and her jeans, revealing that she had an infinity symbol tattoo on her ankle. I recorded all these and waited for my future to unfold. Robin and I became engaged later that year. I knew nothing about signs at that time – I just asked for something to confirm the strong intuition I had that I'd already met my husband.

Although I had already evolved to leaving space for the unexpected on my action boards, as I realised there might be things I could achieve that I could not yet comprehend and I didn't want to be limited by my own brain, this was one of the first times I understood that it's not possible to control and plan everything. In fact, there's something else that you can tap into that is influencing what happens in your life. I was clearly already looking for signs to interpret and guide my intuition, and I now believe that advert and the infinity symbols were signs that aligned with my intentions, as the action board also included a picture of an engagement ring. If I hadn't been so in tune with my intuition in the first place, I might have missed the signs telling me that Robin was my twin flame.

In Chapter 2, we saw that intuition is an undervalued but important source of wisdom, both in terms of us using the full range of decision-making tools at our disposal, and also when it comes to being open to signs in the first place and then understanding them when they do arrive. I now want to delve a bit deeper and explain where intuition lies and why it is so important that you appreciate its physical and sensory aspect, as this will enable you to access your intuition more easily. If you then open yourself up to what your intuition is telling you, who knows what signs you might receive or where they might guide you. In this chapter, we will look at how you can access this great source of wisdom to help you better notice and interpret your signs.

Where Is Intuition?

To me, intuition is knowing in your mind that something's the right thing to do and also feeling it in your body. Perhaps you've used the expressions 'That just gave me chills', 'That gave me goosebumps' or 'I felt it in my gut'? Or maybe, in response to sad or unexpected news, you've had a visceral reaction, such as your stomach tightening, breaking into a sweat or a shiver running down your spine? That's because sometimes we feel something on a physical rather than just a cognitive level. However, our minds and bodies work together, so the intuitive power of them being aligned or in harmony is greater than either on its own.

Although intuition is sometimes referred to as gut instinct, I still think that people think of intuition as a solely mental rather than physical process. But, as we saw in Chapter 2, 'gut instinct' is a good term for it, because it's thought that we store unconscious memories deeper even than the most primal areas of the brain, in our spinal cord, gut neurons and perhaps even our fascia or connective tissue, although the latter remains a speculative hypothesis for the time being.[1] Also, the skin is our largest organ, and there is a strong psychological connection with it, as it is not just the physical boundary of our bodies but is also connected to our mental states. The field of study that researches this is called psychodermatology. So, just as psychological issues can show up as rashes or other skin issues, the hairs on your skin standing on end could be a positive signal from your intuition. If you can access this store of embodied wisdom and use it in conjunction with your brain, then it's stronger than just thinking something in your head.

The main evidence for this comes from studies done on the impact of trauma on the body. In his seminal book *The Body Keeps the Score*, Bessel van der Kolk shares his years of research on this subject, describing how traumatic events leave a physical as well as a mental imprint on us.[2] I experienced this deep connection between the physical and mental at approximately the ten-month point after Robin's death – I was doing better than I had been for a long while, but I knew the first anniversary of his passing was coming up on 26 October, so I was trying to mentally prepare myself for it. Then, from 4 October, I had terrible aches and pains all over my body, and I couldn't work out why. I eventually looked through my phone calendar and discovered that 4 October 2021 was the day I had taken Robin home for the last time, knowing that he only had a matter of weeks to live. The physical pain I was feeling lasted for six or seven weeks and was accompanied by me feeling deeply depressed. That's when I realised that although I hadn't mentally remembered the anniversary of taking him home for the last time, it was an incredibly stressful and poignant day, so perhaps my body had somehow remembered it, because suddenly all this pain had manifested. I had allowed the tension in my muscles to build up, and the reason I felt such pain beginning on 4 October was because I hadn't done enough to deal with the physical aspects of my grief. I have now come to think that this pain may have been my trauma surfacing and eventually exiting my body.

It works two ways: just as the mind can manifest physiological effects, the physical sensations and movements of the body can also affect the mind. That's why van der Kolk's research shows that trauma held in the body can be released through somatic therapies.[3] Somatic means 'of the living body' and relates to the mind–body exchange. Somatic therapies are therefore techniques that focus on physical rather than verbal actions. So, for example, post-traumatic stress disorder (PTSD) doesn't necessarily resolve as effectively if you only do mental work, such as talking therapies, because you're not processing the trauma in the body. Contrary to psychosomatic symptoms (physical symptoms caused by anxiety and worry), this trauma does not necessarily lead to physical manifestations, but it can't be processed fully without a physical element.

In an interview, the renowned physician Gabor Maté emphasised this point. He said: 'Physiologically, you can't separate the mind from the body. Our emotional circuits, the immune system, the hormonal apparatus and the nervous system are actually one system. So, when things happen emotionally, naturally they have a physiological effect.' He then went on to give a number of examples, including the fact that children whose parents are stressed are much more likely to have asthma, women with severe PTSD have double the risk of ovarian cancer, and adults who experience the loss of an adult child have a higher risk of malignancy of the bone marrow and blood. He explained that this has been known for a long time: 'Two thousand four hundred years ago, Socrates, the Greek philosopher, said that the problem with the doctors of today is that they separate the mind from the body.'[4]

I believe that van der Kolk's theory can be taken even further: just as trauma can be held in the body, so too can wisdom and knowledge that we can access for the purposes of healing and intuitive guidance. In my previous book, *The Source*, I explained that journalling was one of the main ways that I was able to access and refine my intuition in the past. However, I have come to realise that this more cerebral approach can only take you so far on its own. The research on alternative approaches to trauma shows us that there are a number of forms of body psychology and other somatic therapies that can provide you with emotional release, healing and intuitive insight in a way that is different to talking therapies or journalling.[5] These include:

- craniosacral therapy
- osteopathy
- acupuncture and acupressure
- body realignment therapy
- reflexology
- tai chi or qigong

I believe that these body therapies also point to the fact that movement and physical exercise are needed in order for us to access the wisdom and deep memories held in our bodies to help inform our intuition. By combining the wisdom held in our bodies with our minds, we can unleash something that is much more powerful than either of those two things alone. It's as if by bringing the two together, instead of choosing one at the expense of the other, we are generating a creative resolution that is greater than the sum of its parts. It's an integrative approach rather than a conventional one.

Practical Ways to Access Your Intuition

You'll see that I have suggested that you do something physical before trying one of the intuition exercises below, although there is an element of the physical, mental, emotional and spiritual in all of what follows. For some, that might be yoga, dancing or drumming, and for others, it might be running or swimming. I have provided some suggestions of beneficial exercises, but, ulti-mately, you need to work out what is best for you, through trial and error or personal recommendation.

Of course, you still need to use your mind to interpret what your body is telling you and make the ultimate decision, but this becomes much easier if you have unlocked this store of intuitive knowledge via some sort of movement or somatic exercise. By doing a physical activity first, and being more in touch with your body, you put yourself in the best position to be able to fully access your intuition.

Physical preparation

You can precede the more cognitive-based exercises with any form of physical activity, whether that's exercise or just simply having a bath or shower. The key thing is that you do both, especially at the beginning as you introduce these practices into your routine for the first time. In the future, you may have established enough of a connection with and understanding of your body that you can do the physical or cognitive exercises on their own and be able to take advantage of your intuition as needed. However, there is something extra powerful about combining them together. Yoga is one of the best things you can do to get your body and mind in sync, so let's start there.

Yoga

Yoga is designed to address the physical, mental, emotional and spiritual aspects of life, thereby providing you with better access to your intuition. Ashtanga, or classical, yoga, for example, strives for the union of mind and body.

It is perhaps not surprising, therefore, that some people find certain physical poses in yoga difficult for mental, emotional or spiritual reasons. For example, van der Kolk has found that people with childhood trauma struggle with happy baby pose (*ananda balasana*). Rosie Underwood, who is an integrative health coach and yoga teacher, says that she typically sees two responses to back-bend poses such as camel pose (*ustrasana*) and wheel pose (*chakrasana*): a sense of euphoria, whereby people feel uplifted, with their hearts open and feeling like they can take on the world; or a sense of vulnerability, whereby people feel exposed and unsupported. The latter is a very primal reaction, as our ancient ancestors wouldn't have exposed their hearts in this way when they were in the wild, because they would have left themselves vulnerable to attack. Back bends can also be difficult if you have experienced a lot of heartbreak or adversity in your lifetime, as there will be a non-conscious desire to protect your heart. And if your brain and heart coherence are out of sync, with the heart wanting one thing and the head another, you will probably find back bends a little bit harder too.

Hip openers, such as pigeon pose (*kapotasana*), can also be quite hard from an emotional and mental point of view. Your primal mind is programmed to predict and prevent, but we live in a very uncertain world, so you can immediately see that there is a conflict there. When you get people with very tight hips, and they find hip openers really hard, it's generally because their mind is in overdrive trying to predict and prevent. In other words, their brains are trying to impose control and garner certainty in an inherently uncertain world. Persevering with hip-opener poses teaches you to let go and surrender a little bit to the unknown and find joy in the beauty of life's mystery. That's perhaps why Rosie finds that people cry a lot when they do hip openers, as they suddenly realise that they can't control everything, which leads to a tremendous sense of mental and emotional release. At the more insidious end of the spectrum, if people don't open their hips when they're very tight, because their minds are trying to exert control, whether consciously or not, it can be indicative of controlling behaviour, perfectionism and even narcissism. This is why it's so important to notice where the body is holding tension and try to release it. Pay attention to this if you practise yoga, and have a think about which poses you struggle with and journal about what that could mean for you.

Dance

Another fundamentally physical practice that I would recommend to help you connect with your body and unlock your intuition is dance; for instance, 5Rhythms, which was developed by Gabrielle Roth in the 1970s. Her philosophy was that everything is made up of energy, which is characterised by waves, patterns and rhythms, so physical movement, specifically dance, can help to alleviate tension in the body and still the mind, almost like a physical form of meditation. The five movements, which are typically done in sequence, are 'flowing', 'staccato', 'chaos', 'lyrical' and 'stillness'.

You probably need to do 5Rhythms in a class led by some-one who knows how to direct you. However, if you want to try something similar yourself, I once did an exercise in an embodied leadership course in which we danced around to the five elements of Chinese ancient wisdom: fire, water, wood, metal and earth. It was a good way to incorporate the physical and the mental, and it is something that anyone can do themselves at home. It might take you outside your comfort zone, but if you can overcome your reticence, I am confident you will feel the benefits.

The aim is to move your body as if you're that substance, and it is very much up to your own interpretation, as there are no prescribed movements. You just need to think, 'If I was made of air, how would I move?', for example. Interestingly, people tend to find some of the elements easier to interpret than others, which can potentially provide a sign as to what issues, mental or physical, they are currently dealing with. For instance, if you found air harder than wood, that might mean that you're a bit rigid and stuck at the moment, or that something is restricting your freedom. In this way, the body releases an intuitive insight into what you are perhaps struggling with, and if you journal about your insights, you might be able to work out what you need to do to move forward.

Gratitude body scan

As I've suggested, you can do yoga, dance, physical exercise or take a bath or shower before moving on to a more cognitive way of accessing your intuition, but I really like this exercise for connecting with your physical self. It is a form of body scan that you can do at any time, although

I find it works well in the shower, as you can actually touch the various parts of the body as you go.

1. Start by touching the top of your head and progressively working your way down your body.

2. Name the part of the body you are touching out loud.

3. Say something positive that you appreciate about that body part – for example, perhaps you like how long or shiny your hair is, or maybe you want to thank your feet for walking you around all day.

4. Once you have moved down your body from head to toe, repeating the process for each body part as you go, turn your attention inward and, one by one, thank your brain and other major organs.

I find this is a wonderful way to feel connected to your body and to understand it a bit better, as you might sometimes come to a part and realise how much more appreciation it deserves.

Intuition exercises

Once you've done some form of physicality or movement, choose one of the following exercises. Do the other on another day after you have again done something to physically prepare yourself.

Yourself in seven years' time

1. Sit in a chair with some clear space in front of you.

2. Formulate a question that expresses something you want or are struggling with at the moment.

3. Describe yourself, saying out loud your name, age and what you're wearing, before articulating the question that you need an answer to.

4. Get up and walk seven steps forward, counting them out as you go, before turning around and looking back at the chair where you were just sitting.

5. Visualise yourself as seven years older than the person you are looking back at, and say your name again and new age – you can even describe what your future self is wearing.

6. Say out loud, 'The answer to your question is . . .' followed by the first thing that comes into your mind.

7. The answer you gave will give you fresh insight from your intuition into whatever it is that you need in the present moment.

This exercise is something I have done myself to great effect, and I've recommended it to lots of friends. Often, it releases some kind of latent emotion, and I and others have found that it can make you cry, which is another good example of how closely our minds and bodies are connected. In fact, you excrete cortisol in your tears, which is why crying can be such an effective stress reliever. Regardless, you should never try to stifle tears, as there are clear benefits to crying and physically releasing emotion from the body.

The unfurling exercise

This is a straightforward but effective exercise that can help you to access information from your entire being, not just your brain.

1. Ask yourself a question or consider a decision that you have to make.

2. Take five deep breaths, put your hands on your head and ask for a logical answer and wait for it to appear.

3. Take five more deep breaths, put your hands on your heart and ask for an emotional answer and wait for it to appear.

4. Take a final five deep breaths, put your hands on your belly and ask for an intuitive answer and wait for it to appear.

If you trust that the first thing that pops into your mind for each step is important in some way, you can then decide which of the answers offers the best option – it could even be that a synthesis of the three answers is the way to go. It is also worth noting that there is a physical element to this exercise despite it being primarily cognitive in nature, as it recognises that knowledge is held in the body as well as the brain, making it a good example of using the two together.

The Gut–Microbiome–Brain Axis

So, we've seen that in order to access your intuition effectively and use it more in your life, you need to unleash the physical store of wisdom held in your body, primarily through movement. But what about this idea of our intuition being held in our gut? What is the basis for this?

In recent years, researchers have shown that 'gut instinct' is not just a figure of speech, and there is emerging evidence that our intuition is in fact related to the bidirectional connection between the gut and the brain. Neurobiological studies have shown that this complex communication system not only ensures the proper maintenance of gastrointestinal homeostasis and digestion, but is likely to have an impact on things such as motivation and higher cognitive functions, including intuitive decision-making.[6] In fact, it's actually a three-way connection between the brain, the gut and the gut microbiome, which is made up of trillions of microbes from hundreds of different species of bacteria that vary depending on what you eat, where you live in the world and what your genetic make-up is.[7] The gut microbiome is therefore unique to each individual, although it may well resemble that of your parents, especially your mother, as vaginal births and breastfeeding are major factors in the seeding of your microbiome. In recent years, as the importance of the gut microbiome to our health and well-being has become clearer, strides have been made to help compensate for when a baby is delivered by Caesarean section or the mother cannot or chooses not to breastfeed.[8] In particular, prebiotics and probiotics are now more commonly added to infant formula to promote the development of a healthy gut microbiome that is more in line with that of breastfed babies.[9] There are also other microbiomes in our bodies, such as the oral and skin microbiomes, but for the purposes of connecting with our intuition we will be focusing on the gut microbiome.

The gut is connected to the brain mainly via nerves in the autonomic nervous system, which, as we've seen, subdivides into sympathetic (fright, fight and flight) and parasympathetic (rest and digest). The vagus nerve (see page 84) has the biggest role in terms of what we know about connecting the gut and the brain, but the intestinal nervous system (which supplies nerve input to all the organs in the abdomen, including the gut) also plays a part in communication between the gut and the brain. The transfer of information between the gut and the brain is also achieved chemically through hormones (for example, from the pancreas) and cytokine messaging (immunological chemical messages that travel in the bloodstream), and via the hormones in the hypothalamic–pituitary–adrenal axis (for example, cortisol), which is a key component of the neuroendocrine (nervous and hormonal) system and contributes to the control of digestion and immune reactions, among many other things.

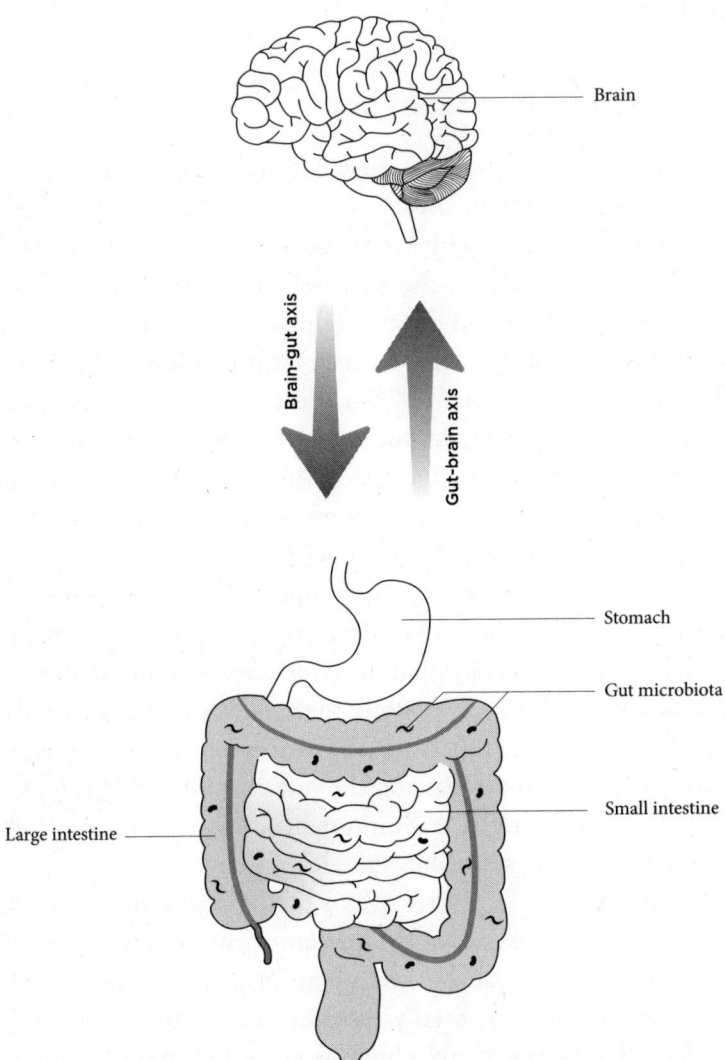

The gut-brain connection

This is perhaps why the gut is often called the second brain, as there is a large network of nerves throughout the gastrointestinal system and in the abdominal organs, and some neurotransmitters are produced in the gut.[10]

Inflammation and brain fog

Nothing in the body operates in isolation, so the functions of the gastrointestinal system also link to the endocrine (hormonal) and immune systems, with 70 per cent of our immune cells held in the gut.[11] Bacteria in the gastrointestinal tract can activate our immune system and deactivate it when it is not needed, the latter helping to avoid unnecessary inflammation and potential autoimmune conditions.[12] When these interlinked systems are inflamed or not in balance, and our gut health is not functioning optimally, we can feel as if access to our intuition is clouded and we cannot trust ourselves, a feeling often referred to as 'brain fog', that many of us can identify with.

There is a lot of evidence to support the role of inflammation in disrupting the gut–brain axis,[13] and impairing mental and emotional processes such as stress, anxiety and depression by inflaming the nerves.[14] While there is less research connecting inflammation, gut–brain axis disruptions and intuition, it is likely happening by impairing the anterior cingulate cortex of the brain, which is key to emotional intuition, and also indirectly by disrupting serotonin signalling.[15]

So, as we saw in Chapter 4, it is really important to manage stress, as stress causes overproduction of cortisol, which erodes our immunity and causes inflammation in our system, particularly in our gut, potentially blocking access to our intuition. Incidentally, the resultant dehydration caused by inflammation can also dry out our skin, hair and entire system, and affect our sleep, as high levels of cortisol can interfere with the release of melatonin (the sleep hormone). This inflammation can show up as bloating or a change in bowel habits, reflux, indigestion, insomnia, skin issues or fatigue and brain fog. Additionally, as we have already seen, many of our emotional and psychological issues show up as physical ailments, like aches and pains or rashes, so taking note of these can alert you to issues in your gut that your conscious mind hasn't identified.

Conversely, if you've got some physical reason why your gut isn't operating as efficiently as usual, your mood could be similarly affected, creating a vicious cycle that can easily snowball, again to the detriment of your intuition. The intestinal tract is lined by a permeable barrier of cells that allows for the absorption of nutrients while also blocking pathogens and foodborne antigens. In this way, it plays a major role in the homeostasis of the gastroenteric system, and if this balance breaks down, it can lead to inflammatory bowel conditions.[16] This in turn means that you can't absorb nutrients in the same way as when your gut is working properly, and therefore the blood supply to the brain isn't fuelling it in the way that is optimal. As a result, the brain again has to allocate what to do with its resources. That's when it goes into 'low-power mode' – the brain will save resources for the things that are absolutely crucial to your survival. Consequently, your mood could suffer, because it's not crucial to your survival to be in a good mood all the time, and things like your emotional regulation, creativity and ability to trust your intuition would be demoted in favour of the essential functions of the brain. This is another reason why it is so important to look after the health of your gut and gut microbiome.

So, if you are suffering from stress, anxiety, depression or insomnia, it has a negative impact on the balance of your gut flora. Equally, if you are malnourished or yo-yo dieting, it affects your mood, concentration, focus and memory, and it can also cloud your access to your intuition. The primary route to fixing brain fog is, therefore, fixing your gut.

Optimising gut health for better intuition

If you can work out for yourself what your body needs, you can make the gut–microbiome–brain system so solid that it provides the foundation for you to build up your intuition, thereby improving your ability to notice and interpret signs.

The good news is that changing your diet can have an almost immediate impact on your gut microbiome, making it one of the biggest health interventions we can instigate ourselves. And there are some obvious signs we can look out for to tell us that our gut microbiome is in need of attention. These include:

- food intolerances

- increased gas and bloating

- changes in bowel movements

- irregular bowel habits

- cramps

- indigestion

- reflux

- change of appetite

- recurring infections or illness

- brain fog

If you do notice any of these changes, or if you just want to aim for optimal gut health, there are a number of things you can do.*

---

* If you notice a more significant change, such as blood in your stools, you should consult your doctor as soon as possible.

Promoting a healthy gut microbiome

Factors that help your gut microbiome thrive include:

- A healthy, balanced diet, focused primarily on plant-based food and fibre.

- A diverse diet – you should aim to eat 30 different plant-based foods a week, including fruit, vegetables, legumes and pulses, herbs and spices, wholegrains, nuts and seeds.

- Probiotic foods such as kefir, kimchi, sauerkraut and kombucha.

- Prebiotic fibre foods such as onion, garlic, artichoke and asparagus.

- Eating foods that are more in step with your cultural heritage – for people with roots in the Indian subcontinent like me, this could be eating coconut products or more spices, whereas someone with a northern European background might be better off eating more seasonal and local produce from that area of the world.

- High-quality probiotic supplements – strains to look out for include *Bifidobacterium longum* and *Lactobacillus brevis*, which have been shown to improve brain cell growth, *Bifidobacterium lactic*, which helps increase immunity, *Lactobacillus plantarum*, which reduces inflammation, and *Lactobacillus gasseri* (CP2305), which helps to reduce cortisol levels and encourages good sleep.[17]

- Drinking plenty of water.

- Aerobic exercise (the evidence suggests benefits despite more research being needed to unpick the reasons why).[18]

- Sufficient length and quality of sleep, with regular sleep and wake times (gut bacteria suffer from jet lag too!). The National Sleep Foundation and other experts recommend seven to nine hours of sleep for adults, although individual needs may vary.[19] More than this can lead to lowered mood and cause metabolic issues such as weight gain and prediabetes. To work out what is best for you, see if you naturally wake up at the same time at weekends as you have to during the week. If you do, you are probably getting enough sleep. If you need to lie in, nap or wish you could sleep all weekend, you are probably not.

- Some psychological therapies such as cognitive behavioural therapy (CBT).[20]

Things to avoid for the health of your gut bacteria include:

- stress

- antibiotics (although sometimes these can't be avoided)

- alcohol

- ultra-processed foods

- smoked foods

- artificial sweeteners

- excessive sugar

- saturated and trans fats

Probiotics

Probiotics have become an increasingly popular way to improve gut health in recent years, but I wouldn't advise that you start taking one without doing some research first. Tim Spector's ZOE project in the UK and similar ones in the USA, like Thrive, allow you to send in stool samples, and they work out exactly which strains of probiotic you personally need to take to best suit the needs of your gut microbiome. The quality of probiotics really matters, too, so it's not just about going to the supermarket and buying a generalised probiotic yoghurt drink, the bacteria in which will most likely be destroyed by your stomach acid. Personalising this process by stool testing or keeping a food, mood and bowel habits diary for one week to work out your baseline is helpful. You can then try a high-quality probiotic supplement for a month and, afterwards, do a food, mood and bowel habits diary for another week to see if it has made a difference. If not, you can try another until you find one that really suits you.

Adaptogens

Another potentially useful strategy for reducing stress to the benefit of your gut microbiome and therefore your intuition is to take an adaptogenic supplement. An adaptogen is an active ingredient in plants or fungi that is non-harmful and helps combat stress and bring the body back to homeostasis.[21] There are a number of adaptogens available, including American ginseng, which can lower stress[22] and boost immunity,[23] Asian ginseng, which can boost mental and physical energy,[24] and Rhodiola rosea, which has antistress and antidepressant properties.[25]

I first came to recognise the benefits of adaptogens at a moment of high stress. I had recently got divorced from my first husband, and I was starting up a new business and had just moved countries, so I did some research to see if there was anything else I could easily incorporate into my routine to help. That's when I discovered that many mushroom varieties have adaptogenic properties. I ordered a bag of mixed mushroom powders, and I felt the benefit almost immediately after I started taking them. Mushroom varieties that have been shown to have adaptogenic qualities include reishi,[26] which has immunomodulating properties, and chaga, which helps to improve energy levels and stave off fatigue.[27]

One mechanism by which adaptogens are thought to work is by a process called adaptive stress response or hormesis, whereby a small amount of stress is introduced into the system that your body can easily adapt to, and this incrementally raises your resilience to stress in the future.[28] By helping to mitigate stress and therefore reduce inflammation, adaptogens potentially have a protective effect on your gut microbiome. In addition to their preventative qualities, studies have shown that they are also effective when taken to alleviate ongoing bouts of stress. One of the most popular adaptogens is ashwagandha, which is taken to increase energy and reduce inflammation, pain and anxiety. A 2019 study showed that a 600mg dose of ashwagandha root extract was most effective in reducing stress levels, as measured by stress and anxiety scales and serum cortisol levels. A 250mg dose was also beneficial but did not show as strong an impact as the higher dosage.[29]

A Tool to Boost Intuition

Once you have laid the groundwork for unfettered access to your intuition by incorporating more movement into your life and ensuring good gut health, you can begin to consciously and deliberately consult your intuition to help you make specific decisions or navigate challenges. To do this, I find it is sometimes helpful to use some sort of device or technique to guide you. For example, one method I find extremely helpful for accessing my intuition is using tarot cards, which I have been fascinated by ever since I first learnt about the fifteenth-century Italian card game *tarocchi*, which later developed into a means of divining the future. However, I use them less out of any sense that they contain mystical power and more as a tool to help me interpret my thoughts and feelings in a more intuitive way with a form of prompt. In his book *The Neuroscience of Tarot*, neuroscientist Siddharth Ramakrishnan makes a very convincing argument for using tarot cards as a tool to hone your intuition.[30]

I have collected a number of different sets of cards over the years, and you can use any type of tarot card, goddess card or angel card, to name but a few. There are lots of methods of reading them, but the following exercise is a simple way to introduce this practice without needing too much background knowledge.

Using tarot cards to access your intuition

1. Take three deep breaths and hold the cards to your chest while calming your mind and asking for guidance.

2. Shuffle the cards, pick three at random and lay them out next to each other, face down.

3. Ask yourself a question or present a dilemma, then turn the cards over and seek an answer from each – you can view them as relating to the past, present and future, if you like.

4. Notice what comes up for you with each card.

5. Most sets come with booklets that explain the traditional meanings of the various cards, but you do not need to read them too literally. Instead, bring

your own interpretations based on what is going on in your life – the most important thing is what the cards mean to you.

6. Make a note of your findings in your journal to see if any of it comes to fruition or makes sense later – by doing so, you will build trust in your interpretations and your ability to think intuitively.

I appreciate that the thought of using tarot or angel cards might be a bit too far 'out there' for some people, and that's fine, as you can still access your intuition in more organic, everyday ways, but even if you are sceptical, I would urge you to give it a go, as it is an excellent way to bring a new perspective to whatever question or problem you might be facing. And if you are finding it hard to access signs, or are early on in the process, tarot cards can be a good way to access your intuition and open yourself up to noticing signs.

Once we have got to a place of understanding what intuition is, and fully appreciate that it is a physical as well as a mental process, we can work to maximise access to it via movement, and by taking good care of our gut microbiomes. This, along with our better awareness of the world thanks to being more in tune with our senses, allows us to take it to the next level and create the best conditions to take advantage of signs, starting with building a better connection with our creativity, which we'll explore next.

KEY TAKEAWAYS

1. Intuition is in your body, not just your mind.
2. Physicality and taking care of the gut–brain axis are vital to honing intuition, giving us better access to a great source of hidden wisdom.
3. Boosting your intuition is key to you accessing your signs.

CHAPTER 6

CONNECT WITH CREATIVITY

The first time I did anything that was in an enclosed space and included a large audience following shielding during the COVID pandemic and then Robin's death was a trip to the ballet. Because I'd been so isolated and had so much health anxiety, I was very nervous about it, but I hoped it would be worth it and, sure enough, when the performance began, I started to cry because I felt so overwhelmed by how beautiful it was. Ballet just seems to speak to my soul.

I've always loved the ballet and, throughout my life, I have been drawn to the theatre. I think the reason I cried was that being back in a theatre watching a beautiful ballet filled me with so much joy and wonder. It also gave me a glimmer of insight that life was still worth living and that there were things I could do to appreciate that and learn how to bring happiness back into my life again.

Many of us think that art, creativity and beauty are frivolous or unessential aspects of life, but nothing could be further from the truth. If we look back at the cultures in which we evolved, we can see that these are, in fact, intrinsic aspects of human existence. Furthermore, science is now showing us that they have tangible mental and physical benefits.[1] This area of research is called neuroaesthetics, and it involves the study of how the arts and creativity impact our brains and bodies, and how that, in turn, can be transferred into practices that help us to grow and thrive.

In this chapter, we will look at how you can harness these benefits, not only for your well-being and longevity, but, just as importantly, to change your mindset and perspective. By doing so, you can heighten your awareness and train your mind to form creative connections, thereby establishing the conditions that allow you to perceive and take advantage of the signs that are meaningful for you.

Beauty Is Essential

We think of art and creativity as nice-to-haves, but actually we know they are integral to tribal cultures – we evolved with them, as a way of understanding the world around us. Although it might not have seemed like they were crucial to our survival, especially when we had scanty resources, the archaeological record reveals to us that ancient humans indulged in creative practices such as cave painting, dancing and humming, to name but a few. Although the precise reasons for this have been lost to the mists of time, we can speculate that our ancestors did this because it helped them to forge bonds with their tribe and environment, and to begin to assign meaning in an uncertain and dangerous world. Extrapolating from studies of modern-day hunter-gatherer societies, we can see that music, for example, is an integral way in which those societies create a framework for their broader understanding of the world.[2] And some anthropologists believe that cave art was a way of recording religious beliefs that could be used to create links between disparate tribal camps, thereby contributing to social cohesion and meaning-making.[3]

Ancient cultures incorporated neuroaesthetic practices into their everyday lives in a very seamless way. When I interviewed Susan Magsamen and Ivy Ross, the authors of *Your Brain on Art*, they told me that many indigenous cultures do not even have a word for 'art', as it's taken for granted that it's central to their lives and culture, in the form of singing, chanting, drumming, storytelling and so on. The multidimensional creativity and culture of the Hopi tribe in the USA is a good example, as it includes the use of totems, food (especially corn), making artefacts, synchronicity with the seasons and nature, ceremonies, rites of passage and so on. And adorning by indigenous peoples, a form of self-expression at its fullest, whether through flowers, feathers, hair braiding, jewellery or painting the body, also shows how important aesthetic practices are.

However, over time, art has gone from something that we recognised as a must-have to a nice-to-have – we have separated it from our being, even though it is in many ways what makes us human. Anthropologist Agustín Fuentes puts forward this idea in his book *The Creative Spark*,[4] arguing that art is embedded deep in prehistory and integral to who we are – in fact, it is what makes us human. In an interview, he said, 'We tend to think of these beautiful cave paintings of the big mastodons and wild oryx as art. But that's only about 40,000 years old.' He then went on to describe some of the earlier known artistic endeavours of our deep ancestors, including carving ostrich eggshells in southern Africa 85,000 years ago, and people wearing shell necklaces and rubbing crumbled ochre onto their bodies 20,000 and 100,000 years respectively earlier than that. 'Five hundred thousand years before that,' he continued, 'they were making tools that were incredibly beautiful and more symmetrical and aesthetic than they had to be to do their jobs.'[5]

In the twenty-first century, many of us have lost sight of this simple fact. With our busy, stressful lifestyles, it's very easy to not bother to adorn ourselves, or to walk past and not notice the flowers, or to not stop to appreciate an impressive piece of architecture, but if we take the time to do so, it can contribute to us thriving and potentially expanding our mental abilities.

The Mind-Bending Benefits of Art

Just like anthropological studies of tribal cultures suggest, the study of neuroaesthetics is demonstrating that art and creativity are beneficial. In the first instance, neuroaesthetics reveals the benefits of being aware of and looking at the beauty that is all around us. Doing so stimulates and therefore enlivens our senses and increases our awareness of the world and the signs that are out there, if only we are open to receiving them. Beholding beauty therefore has something of a dual benefit: on the one hand, a beautiful piece of art can have meaning for us, but on the other hand, it enhances our ability to see and draw upon signs more generally. It's definitely done so for me.

In addition to beholding beauty, neuroaesthetics has also studied the benefits of making and participating in creative pursuits, whether that's sketching, playing an instrument or writing poetry. And the good news is that your skill level does not equate to the benefits you get from those neuroaesthetic practices – simply being creative, in whatever form works for you, is going to be beneficial to you in lots of meaningful ways. In fact, there are neurological advantages to both making and beholding. Creative practice engages neural pathways, lowers cortisol, activates the parasympathetic nervous system, lowers stress, manages anxiety and impulse control, and builds resilience.[6] Beholding, meanwhile, such as watching theatre or ballet, helps us to synchronise with others, promotes empathy and provides perspective, as well as shifting the brain towards an oxytocin state of joy and excitement.[7]

Lowers your mortality risk

There are longevity benefits too: a study showed that people who engage in the arts every few months – for example, by going to the theatre or visiting a museum – have a 31 per cent lower risk of dying. Even if you only go once or twice a year, your risk of mortality is lowered by 14 per cent.[8] I find this pretty astonishing, and with many publicly funded galleries and museums being free of charge, it seems like a no-brainer to me that we should try to incorporate these sorts of activities into our lives wherever possible.

One of the potential mechanisms for this lowering of mortality rate is similar to the benefits you get from gratitude practices,[9] as they create emotions such as joy, love, trust and excitement that cannot coexist with fear, anger, disgust, shame or sadness, so this means less cortisol and subsequently less inflammation throughout the body. Inflammation is the leading cause of many chronic diseases and poses a significant threat to health and longevity.[10] At a more emotional or spiritual level, art and creativity lead to feelings of freedom, peace, connection and ultimately transcendence. And living without fear and stress leads to greater creativity, more flexible thinking, the ability to solve problems and the suppression of biases.

Boosts your mental state

The benefits we gain from beauty and creativity are not just neural or psychological processes; there's a chemical reaction to art and beauty, too, with the body releasing dopamine, oxytocin, serotonin and endorphins, sometimes referred to as the 'DOSE' hormones, which have a variety of functions:

- Dopamine – heavily involved in motivation, goal-setting and reward anticipation. It's released when we achieve small wins, making us want to continue.

- Oxytocin – contributes to bonding and is released when we feel joy, excitement, love and trust.

- Serotonin – regulates mood, long-term motivation and confidence.

- Endorphins – natural painkillers and mood boosters.

If you're suffering from grief or feeling depressed or negative, you can have talking therapy or body realignment therapy to relieve some of this and try to heal, but an accompaniment to this might be to boost the DOSE hormones in your system through art, beauty and creativity. Appreciating beauty shifts the brain from a fear state (cortisol) to a love/trust state (oxytocin), also moving our autonomic nervous system from sympathetic to parasympathetic, which further helps us to access hitherto clouded intuition and a willingness to take healthy risks.

Stimulates neuroplasticity

Not only can art and creativity lower stress, they can also shape your brain in positive ways. When our sensory systems are ignited by creativity and beauty, it leads to neuroplasticity changes by exposing our brains to the new ways of thinking that beauty and creativity promote, thereby forging new neural pathways. Appreciating beauty is potentially a good way, therefore, of getting rid of the undesired neural connections created by repeated negative thoughts. Art and beauty create the environment for your brain to be more filled with joy, leaving little room for fear and doubt. Positive affirmations or mantras are also helpful in this regard. You are then much more likely to be in a good mood and confident and motivated to see your signs.

However, as we saw in Chapter 2, most of the time we naturally filter out things that aren't essential to our survival, which can be as simple as not stopping and appreciating a beautiful sunset or public sculpture. You need to shift your brain to notice those things, even if they're not essential to your survival, because they will ultimately help you to flourish. You may not notice something that is actually important to you if you are not directing your attention to it in a deliberate way.

In *Your Brain on Art*, Susan and Ivy argue that beholding art is one of the best ways to boost and fine-tune your saliency network (see page 38), because you are more likely to notice something beautiful, provocative, surprising or new and understand what this means for you, moving you away from habituation.[11] It therefore pays to introduce novelty into your life and to be curious and open-minded, as this will expand your awareness and perception. It's a two-way thing: if you are open and curious, you will notice more beautiful things, and if you expose yourself to appreciating beauty, you'll induce greater saliency and neuroplasticity than somebody who doesn't expose their brain to new and varied stimuli. By incorporating art, beauty and creativity in your life, you essentially train your brain to notice more, and this will in turn make you more highly attuned to noticing and interpreting signs.

Cultivating beauty in your life

Set yourself a journal challenge to record ten things you noticed during the day that inspired awe or beauty in you. This is a nice wind-down routine when you start to relax in the evenings.

Brings you into the present moment

The realisation that the benefits of artistic or creative practice are not linked to how skilled you are at whatever creative endeavour you are undertaking was a game-changer for me. There's something quite refreshing about being creative and having no expectation of it being perfect or even good, necessarily. You just take enjoyment out of it. Because so many aspects of our lives are filled with pressure to perform and achieve and be the best that we can be, sometimes it's nice to be more in the moment and do something just for the sake of doing it, and when you're experiencing awe, when you're beholding beauty, when you're immersed in music, you are also very present. I definitely feel a lot of pressure for my work to be perfect, so doing something like playing the piano keyboard, which I know is not one of my strongest skills but I still enjoy it, is putting my brain in a very different state, one that it's not in very much.

This brain state is a form of mindfulness or mind wandering where you are more likely to make connections that you don't when switched on and busy. Although I am concentrating and putting in effort, I get lost in the moment – this is sometimes referred to as 'flow'. For you, this could be achieved through singing to manage emotions or colouring in mandalas as a form of mindfulness to reduce anxiety.

Sometimes the signs you've received only make sense when you are doing something that places you in another zone, such as the 'Eureka!' moment of Archimedes realising while in the bath that he could measure the volume of an irregular shape by the amount of water it displaced, or Paul McCartney coming up with the melody for 'Yesterday' in his dreams. These things happen when they are not part of your conscious process and you have stopped thinking about them. The same is true of signs – sometimes the interpretation of something's relevance or meaning comes together in an unrelated moment of insight. For instance, you might see something that you intuitively feel is a sign and then only days later realise its meaning.

Provides psychological safety

When you perform or share something you've made, you also put yourself in quite a vulnerable position, and it can therefore be a bit daunting. However, it is hugely beneficial, as this vulnerability opens you up to new experiences and exposes you to a little bit of risk in a safe environment. Psychological safety is feeling that you can express yourself fully, and expressing yourself, being creative and enlivening your sensory system are all benefits of creativity that neuroaesthetics reveals to us, as they all contribute to enhanced well-being and a deeper connection with the world around you. This feeling of safety then allows you to express yourself, get out of your comfort zone and explore more fully all that life has to offer, including signs from beyond. Knowing that you can learn and do new things, particularly creative ones because of the beneficial effects they have on your brain, is part of the journey to believing your mind is capable of much more than you think it is right now.

To summarise, the arts, creativity and beauty lower stress and can help to manage anxiety, therefore boosting resilience and flexibility. They also bring you into the present moment and improve the art of noticing. This has benefits in and of itself, and also contributes to you being able to notice signs and open your mind to them.

I feel like the way I engage with the world now has completely changed my appreciation of beauty – and not only in the traditional sense of the word. If I wake up and know it is going to be a challenging day, apart from my gratitude practice – where I give thanks for my bed, bedding, silk pillowcase and so on – I think to myself, 'What am I going to see that's beautiful today?' Or, 'Where am I going to go that has beauty?' This is a simple way of ensuring that I am prioritising art and creativity in my life, especially at times when I am in even more need of the fortification they bring. I am also much more conscious of observing beauty whenever I can and in the least expected things. The other day, as I was leaving my house, I noticed that the two pots of lavender at my front door were looking particularly healthy and full of life. I stopped for a moment and thought, 'Oh my goodness, the lavender is looking amazing,' but I had some-where to be so didn't dwell for too long. However, when I came back, I deliberately stopped and looked at the plants properly, really taking in their shape and colour, and deeply breathing in their scent. It was a small moment, but it was a way of appreci-ating the beauty around me more fully and with intentionality, which is important when it comes to engaging the brain. In the past, I might not have done that so consciously and proactively.

As I've said, I've always loved the arts and culture, but I now realise that I actually don't thrive without it, and I was never aware of that before. Being more creative has led to a willingness to have conversations I might not have had before, and I'm more open to challenge than I ever was before. I'm also more flexible now and open to change. So, tapping into the ben-efits revealed by neuroaesthetics has had a positive impact on other areas of my life beyond being more creative and aware of beauty, and embracing it could do the same for you.

Bringing Art and Creativity into Your Life

Bringing beauty into your life is not just about going to the ballet or an art gallery. Many of us have come to believe that art is somehow elitist and only for a small section of society, but as Susan and Ivy told me when I interviewed them, it is in fact a basic human need and everyone's birthright, and I believe we should all see beauty and creativity as being accessible to us.

I want to stress that it is not the case that you can only be happier and healthier if you can afford really expensive art or tickets to high-end cultural performances. Instead, you can listen to music, read a book or poem, or display your children's paintings on the fridge. Similarly, you don't need to buy expensive art supplies or sign up for a ten-week dance or music class if you want to be more creative – all you need if you want to start drawing is a pencil and a piece of paper, and you can dance around your living room or sing in the shower at no cost at all. If you can then regularly incorporate these small acts into your daily life, you can take advantage of the power of incremental change that micro-habits offer, as I mentioned in the opener to Part 2 (page 74).

Despite the benefits of art and creativity, and the fact that we can bring them into our lives in everyday ways, a lot of the people I work with and teach, when asked, say that they aren't creative. However, when I describe creativity from a scientific point of view – namely, seeing patterns that aren't obvious to others and joining the dots when it's not always easy to – the response is more often than not, 'Oh, in that case, I'm definitely creative.' The reality is that we all have the ability to be creative in one way or another, and it is important that we embrace this aspect of our lives in order to benefit from the stress-lowering and salience-boosting qualities of art and creativity. Below are some ways that you can incorporate beauty and creative practice into your life.

Adorn yourself

What clothes you choose to put on each day might not seem obviously relevant here, but how you dress and what colours you wear can be forms of creative expression. Pink is my favourite colour, and if I'm presenting at a conference, for example, I'll tend to wear something pink, red or purple to be unashamedly feminine, even in a scientific or academic world. On the flip side, I remember saying to someone in the first year or two after Robin died that I was wearing a lot of grey, navy and black, and I just didn't feel like wearing pink because it didn't really feel like a representation of the emotions I was feeling. I would encourage you to be emboldened to wear the clothes and accessories, hairstyles and make-up that express who you are, and don't be afraid to be creative in your choices.

Surround yourself with beauty

Some of the ways that I incorporate beauty into my life include listening to classical music and going to art galleries. I also like to have beautiful art and objects in my house – Robin and I chose a lot of art, textiles such as Persian carpets, books and furniture together – and having a vibrant and stimulating garden is an extension of this.

If you seek out and surround yourself with beautiful things, you're much more likely to create an environment in which you feel psychologically safe to trust yourself, take healthy risks and notice the signs that can guide you. And those beautiful things don't have to be expensive. You could pick flowers from your garden and put them in a vase or glass. If I get squashes or pumpkins in my veg box, I put them somewhere around my house because I think they look charming. They don't need to be kept in the fridge, and they last for a long time, so I instead place them on a windowsill or next to some books on my coffee table, especially in the autumn. By doing so, I'm not just adding something pleasant into my environment, I'm also introducing an element of novelty, because you wouldn't expect to find an interesting-looking pumpkin sitting on a table in your living space. And because novelty is one of the main ways that we create fresh neural pathways, there is an additional benefit to displaying them in this way beyond their decorative value. It also makes me smile, and visitors often comment on it.

Think about ways in which you could bring beauty into your own environment. Again, this does not necessarily mean spending lots of money. You can pick up and display beautiful shells or pine cones in your home, and moss bowls have become very popular, all of which are examples of bringing touches of nature indoors (more of which in the next chapter).

Try music, chanting or humming

Music is one of the most impactful ways to incorporate art and creativity into your life, and this is again something that humans have known for millennia. Ancient cultures such as the Aboriginal Australians, for example, recognised the benefits of music and vibration on their well-being and carved instruments that create strong vibrations, such as the didgeridoo. Even if you are just listening rather than playing, you can feel the vibrations in your body. The ancient Buddhist practice of manipulating sound bowls also creates noise and vibrations simultaneously. Sound bowls have had a real resurgence recently, and gong baths and sound healing are now very popular because of the restful impact they are said to have on your nervous system.

Of course, not everyone has access to a didgeridoo or would want to learn how to use one, but you can go to a singing bowl class or do some drumming at home to recreate a similar effect, and the benefits include moving your brainwave state more towards the alpha or gamma states* and boosting

* Brainwaves refer to the electrical functioning of the brain, in which there are five main states: alpha, which is associated with deep relaxation while awake; beta, which is associated with normal brain function while awake; delta, which is associated with the deepest levels of sleep; gamma, which is associated with the fastest brain activity and advanced cognitive functioning such as learning and memory; and theta, which is associated with daydreaming and light sleep.

neurotransmitters and hormones, leading to improved mood, reduced anxiety, pain relief, improved sleep, and enhanced mental clarity and body awareness.[12] Being in those brainwave states can either induce deep relaxation or enhance your cognitive abilities, both of which are conducive to you receiving signs (like the 'Eureka!' moments mentioned previously). Vibration and humming also cause the release of nitric oxide in our cells, which helps to expand our blood vessels and therefore increase blood flow and decrease blood pressure. As such, it can help to reduce stress, allowing us to access our intuition and creativity more easily.[13]

It's not just vibrating instruments that are beneficial, though. Playing any instrument is valuable as it engages almost every part of the brain, including those that help us to process movement, sensation, hearing, seeing and emotion. The advantages of learning an instrument can last a lifetime and be impactful even if you start in your sixties or older. These include protecting memory and cognition as we age, promoting neuroplasticity, improving executive functions such as decision-making, and generating a higher concentration of grey matter (neurons) and synapses.[14] However, despite there being benefits to playing an instrument at any age, the earlier you get started the better – musicians who began musical training before the age of seven have been shown to have a larger corpus callosum, the bridge that connects the two hemispheres of the brain.[15] This creates more interconnection and boosts executive functions such as complex problem-solving, creative thinking and cognitive flexibility.

If you do not already play an instrument and don't have the time or inclination to learn one from scratch, you can still be musical by humming or singing along to the radio. And even just listening to music is beneficial to us, particularly if it brings us joy or moves us.

Dance

Dance is also good for your mental health, and has been shown to be one of the most effective forms of physical activity for treating depression, although more research remains to be done on this, particularly with regard to male and older participants, as most of the studies have so far focused on younger women.[16] Dance is also an excellent way to tune in to your senses and connect to your body, thereby enhancing your ability to notice signs (as we saw in Chapter 4).

Cook

There are, of course, a multitude of things that we can do that are less obviously creative. For example, I love cooking, which for me has always been a creative and extremely therapeutic outlet. When I know that I have a busy day coming up, I'll sometimes prep my food the night before or in the morning so that I can really enjoy cooking it in the evening, which in turn helps me to relax. And not only is it something that I'm passionate about, it also acts on and stimulates multiple senses simultaneously. Somebody once said that the first bite is with the eye. If I go to a restaurant and the food is really beautifully prepared, I definitely notice that, and it makes me happy. Experiencing joy, appreciating beauty and recalling memories associated with these events contribute to your personal development via neuroplasticity.

Is there something in your life that might not immediately seem artistic but that nonetheless brings with it the benefits of being creative? If yes, embrace it as being creative, and try to prioritise it more. As I said above, creativity is a way of thinking as much as anything.

Paint, draw or craft

The benefits of painting, drawing and crafts have been demonstrated by Bessel van der Kolk, who has conducted extensive research into people with PTSD using art as a therapeutic tool, and also to track their progress through therapy.[17] In one of his experiments, he asked the participants to draw a picture of their families every week, and the pictures went from being very vague and rough to being drawn with much more care and attention to detail, thereby demonstrating the participants' progress. Painting, drawing and making crafts are actually very mindful tasks, as they require you to observe and focus on the present moment and the creative process. This can help to quiet the mind and reduce stress.[18] Creative activities such as these are also forms of self-expression, which can be a powerful tool for processing emotions and raising self-awareness.[19]

Drawing your signs

Try adding drawings of your signs to your journalling practice, rather than just writing. This is a simple way to track your progress with receiving signs.

Read for pleasure

One of the most accessible creative practices you can bring into your life is reading for pleasure. While most of us would probably agree that writing is a creative practice – some would even say it is an art form in the hands of our most talented writers – it might not seem immediately obvious that reading is one too. However, reading novels strengthens the connections between different parts of the brain,[20] and it has been shown to promote empathy.[21] Studies have also shown that it can positively affect your mental health and well-being if it is reinforced by reflection and, even better, discussing what you have read with others – in this way, joining a book club is not just something fun to do, it might also help to improve your mental health.[22] More anecdotally, reading for pleasure can engage your imagination, and it enhances creativity by introducing you to new knowledge, ideas, perspectives and cultures. In this way, reading is also another excellent way in which you can broaden your horizons, therefore creating the space for an expanded conception of what is possible, including gaining access to signs from beyond. I would therefore encourage you to put down your screen and pick up a book as often as you can.

After Robin died and I eventually had the mental capacity and desire to read again, I decided to start working my way through various books he had bought me that I had not got round to reading previously, as this made me feel some connection to him. These were both fiction and non-fiction, as he kept track of the work-related topics I was interested in. I felt more drawn to the novels, so I read *Hamnet* by Maggie O'Farrell. It was a grief story, which I was not aware of before I started reading it, and Robin had bought it for me a long time before he even became unwell, so it was a coincidence that I picked it up during my ongoing grief. In *Hamnet*, Shakespeare tragically loses his only son, and the novel recounts the unravelling of a family distraught with grief and torn apart by being unable to understand each other's coping mechanisms. Towards the end, Shakespeare's wife witnesses a new play he has written named for their son in which a young actor with a striking resemblance to him delivers the last line: 'Remember me.' The effect this has on her gave me chills, and I felt there was definitely a message for me in there from Robin. I also felt it was a sign of something that I already believe, which is that the right book finds you at the right time – a way

I have found of feeling less guilty about my ever-increasing pile of unread books.

In this novel and others that I still have not read, I also rediscovered handwritten messages from Robin from all those birthdays, Christmases and anniversaries that I had not seen for a long time – another deep source of comfort and reassurance for me during some dark times. I feel that I was meant to find them at that time, showing that the signs you need will find you if you are open to receiving them. I truly believe that if you allow moments of easy creativity into your life, such as reading, signs will come to you and show you a way forward.

Prioritising creativity

Creative practices are so varied, and each individual will have their own personal preference, so I will leave it up to you what you choose to do, but the following exercise is a good way of finding the space for it in your life, whatever it is.

1. Spend some time thinking about an activity you do habitually that is not necessarily serving you – one of the most obvious examples for many of us today is scrolling through social media.

2. Decide which creative practice you want to have a go at – this can be something you already love but don't find time to do often enough, or it can be something completely new.

3. Replace the unhelpful activity with the creative one for 30 minutes to one hour each day for a week.

4. At the end of the week, have a think about whether you feel any better for having replaced the negative activity with something creative, and journal about the results

so you can refer back to them later if the creative pursuit lapses.

5. Try to make space for the creative activity in your life from that point onwards.

As humans, we don't just want to manage or cope; we want to thrive and flourish. Art and creativity help prepare us to reach our full potential, as they point to a deeper, richer way to feel fully human.

But it's also important not to force things or push yourself too hard. At the beginning of the first COVID lockdown, the instinct of many of us was that we could use the imposed pause in our lives to learn a new language, say, or start a creative business. However, I remember thinking that we should first and foremost look after ourselves and not apply too much pressure, because if the pandemic turned out to be really stressful, which it was for many people, the last thing we should be doing was trying to learn something new and challenging, thereby ramping up the pressure even more. My approach has always been that if you're under stress, you should stick to your normal routine, and the time to learn new things and take some risks is when you are in a better mental state and have sufficient bandwidth.

It's almost as if you need a volume dial. When you're stressed, you need to do less intensive creative things, such as listening to your favourite music or looking at some art. If you're not stressed, you can take it to a level where it's bit more challenging, like drawing or playing an instrument. Depending on where are you mentally, think about the things you can do to help you either survive or thrive.

As I've said, it's all too easy to forego beauty and creativity, to label them as frivolous and not essential, whereas the opposite is actually true, as our ancestors realised. Without that understanding of how important they are, you might be overlooking them and therefore missing out on the benefits they can provide to your brain–body system, including less stress and a boost to your saliency network. If you are more alert and able to slow down and be in the moment as a result of these benefits, you can direct your general awareness of the world in a more deliberate way, opening up the possibility of noticing other signs, including from your immediate environment, especially nature, which is the focus of the next chapter.

KEY TAKEAWAYS

1. The arts and creativity have mental and physical health benefits.
2. Being good at art is irrelevant to the benefits it can bring to your life.
3. Noticing and appreciating beauty primes your brain to see and interpret signs.

CHAPTER 7

CONNECT WITH NATURE

Do you have a place in nature that feels special to you? Throughout my life, whenever I was confronted with a life-changing dilemma, I would go for a walk and sit and reflect on Hampstead Heath, because it's the place where I can best access my intuition. It's very special to me, because I grew up around there and went regularly as a child, and I feel like it's got some kind of spiritual energy, more than just a normal park, perhaps because it is less manicured and wilder than most other urban green spaces. Similarly, whenever my friends say to me that they're struggling with their mood or mindset, I always recommend they go for a walk in nature. I believe you always notice the benefit of walking in a park or by a river, and my friends invariably report back that they really did feel better afterwards.

But what is the reason for this? According to Susan Magsamen and Ivy Ross, 'the ultimate enriched environment is nature'.[1] In other words, one of the most important environments in terms of our well-being, and also when it comes to our ability to access signs, is nature. Again, this is something that we once knew but have lost sight of, particularly in industrialised Western societies. Ancient civilisations were more attuned to nature and the information their environments provided about how to live their lives. This knowledge was passed down from generation to generation but has been largely lost today, as these oral traditions were not recorded. However, I believe we can reclaim some of this knowledge by looking to ancient cultures for inspiration.

The spaces we inhabit have a profound impact on our health and well-being on the one hand, and our ability to engage with life on a deeper level on the other. However, for the most part, we are not consciously aware of the effect our environments are having on us. For example, our bodies and brains can react very differently to an environment – you might think you like a particular shade of paint on the wall, but it could actually be triggering a stress response in your body as a result of some negative association from the past. This is why having a greater awareness of your environmental influences is so important. If you can reconnect with nature, you can lower stress and create a sense of calm and connectedness in your otherwise hectic life that will help you to notice and interpret the signs that come to you with more ease.

The Profound Impact of Our Environments

During the COVID pandemic, when many people around the world found themselves in lockdown, the quiet streets and empty skies allowed many of us to reconnect with nature, and just for a moment it seemed like we might have the chance to recalibrate our relationship with the natural world. However, it didn't take long for us to revert to our old habits and retreat back into our urban, technology-driven lives. This was a missed opportunity, because our connection with nature is much more important than many of us realise.

The fact that our environments have a huge impact on us far beyond what most of us appreciate was aptly demonstrated by a number of seminal experiments conducted on rats in the early 1960s, in which neuroscientist Marian Diamond and her research team discovered that the brain is not fixed from birth and can in fact grow and change throughout the course of our lives.[2] This was the birth of the concept of neuroplasticity, the theory that has been so central to my life and work. In the original experiment, one group of rats was kept in a neutral, unchanging environment to act as the control, another was placed in an enriched environment, including a rotating range of toys, thereby introducing interest and novelty, and the third was placed in a basic environment with no source of mental stimulation. The group in the enriched environment showed neuroplasticity changes in their brains, demonstrated by a 6 per cent growth in their cerebral cortices as compared to those in the group in the deprived environment, which had actually lost brain mass. Not only did this shocking and paradigm-shifting discovery overturn a deeply held scientific conviction that the brain is unchanging, it also pointed to the importance of external stimulation and the environments we place ourselves in. Diamond is now considered to be one of the founders of modern neuroscience.[3]

Diamond's experiments demonstrated that our environments have an influence on us, and that a sense of enrichment can lead to neuroplasticity changes in the human brain too. You are signalling to yourself all the time by creating the environment that you spend most of your time in, and this has an effect on your physiology through your senses. But your environment will influence you regardless of whether you're conscious of and curating and enriching it or not. In other words, it'll still act upon you, but not necessarily to your benefit.

If you actively engage with your environment and nature, you can optimise your brain to operate at a higher level, and also to notice even more signs. If I said to you that, like the rats in Marian Diamond's experiments, your brain is now 6 per cent bigger than it was this time last year, what would you do with that? You could become better at your job, but you could also use that extra brainpower to expand your whole way of living by noticing the signs that guide you towards whatever you want.

The fact that our environments can elicit responses that we might not expect or realise is not just conjecture – it has been demonstrated in an experimental context. In 2019, Ivy Ross, in her role as vice president of hardware design at Google, partnered with New York-based architect Suchi Reddy and the International Arts + Mind Lab at the Johns Hopkins University School of Medicine's Brain Science Institute, run by Susan Magsamen, to create the *A Space for Being* exhibit at the Salone del Mobile (Milan Design Week), an annual international furniture fair in Milan. Participants were invited to spend some silent time in three carefully curated spaces. Each room was set up to provide calming but very different sensory experiences, with a variety of colours, textures, sounds and smells. Before entering the spaces, visitors were given special wristbands developed by Google that measured a range of biometrics, including heart rate, breathing rate, skin temperature and body motion. At the end of the experience, a user's physiological response was analysed, and a private printout generated that showed the rooms in which the person had felt most calm and where their response had been heightened. About half the users, when asked, said that the findings corresponded with what they expected – in other words, their psychological responses matched their physiological responses. However, in the other half there was a mismatch, demonstrating that our environments can have an impact on us beyond our conscious awareness. After the event, Ross said, 'What we really wanted to do was give people a mirror to reflect back to themselves the fact that the body is always feeling, and sometimes it might even be different from what your mind is thinking.'[4]

Saskia Wheeler is a neuroaesthetics consultant, and she explained to me that the spaces we inhabit, whether at home, at work or in the wider world, can have a significant impact on our stress levels in particular and negatively impact on our ability to access signs by placing us in a sympathetic rather than para-sympathetic state (see page 92). For example, rooms with lots of wooden surfaces have been shown to reduce stress and lower blood pressure compared to ones with lots of metal and sharp edges.[5] Similarly, neuroaesthetic research shows that being in or viewing enclosed spaces can heighten feelings of anxiety. Researchers investigating the impact of ceiling height and our reaction to being in an enclosed space showed in brain scans that when we are exposed to enclosed spaces, the amygdala, which regulates anxiety, sends information to the anterior midcingulate cortex, which plays a role in regulating emotions to prevent incorrect automatic threat responses, monitoring of conflict, processing emotionally relevant stimuli, learning, memory and decision-making. And they act together to view the environment as a potential threat.[6] This is something that we see throughout the animal kingdom, with enclosed spaces often being avoided as they may be impossible to escape from when we are faced with a threat. As a result, curved shapes and open spaces, perhaps because they are evocative of nature, can promote feelings of safety and warmth.[7] If we want a more posi-tive interaction with our environments, it is, therefore, to nature that we should turn.

Nature is the most impactful environment

Humans have evolved into what we are today over the course of approximately 6–7 million years. If we define the beginning of urbanisation as the Industrial Revolution, less than 0.004 per cent of our history has been spent in modern surroundings. It's no surprise, then, that having spent the vast majority of our time as a species living in nature, our physiological functions are highly adapted to this environment, or that the urbanised and artificial settings that most of us inhabit now are contributing factors to the high levels of stress that we see today.

Because the majority of human existence has been spent in nature, it is the most aesthetically pleasing and calming environment for most of us, as well as enlivening our sensory systems via scent, sound, colour and texture. As a result, there are common physiological responses among all humans to landscapes, because an appreciation and connection with nature is innate.

For example, time in nature lowers cortisol levels, indicating stress reduction, makes us feel more present and grounded, and lowers our cognitive loads. One study in urban nature spaces showed that the duration of time spent in nature correlated with the amount of stress reduction. When the duration of the 'nature dose' was between 20 and 30 minutes, the gain in benefit was seen to be most efficient.[8]

As a result, it has become increasingly common for time in nature to be prescribed by medical professionals, as it has been shown to be an effective and cost-efficient way to improve mental health. A major government-backed scheme helping more than 8,000 people in England to connect with nature (via nature walks, wild swimming, community gardening and tree planting) led to big improvements in anxiety, depression, happiness and the feeling that life was worthwhile.[9] Another study showed that a 90-minute walk in nature led to decreased activity that is often associated with depression in the subgenual prefrontal cortex.[10]

These sorts of nature-based practices are often collectively referred to as forest bathing, which is said to originate from the Japanese art of *Shinrin-yoku*, and they have been shown to have psychological and physiological benefits. In particular, studies have demonstrated that forest bathing and urban green space therapy decrease levels of salivary cortisol, pulse rate and blood pressure, and markers used to measure parasympathetic nervous activity increase while markers demonstrating sympathetic nervous activity decrease. Other factors tested were wooden material therapy and plant therapy through tactile stimulation (touching natural substances such as wood or foliage), olfactory stimulation (smelling cypress wood or orange essential oil) and visual stimulation (being in a room with a wooded wall or looking at fresh roses).[11] These factors induced a state of physiological relaxation, and it is in this state that we are more open to perceiving and interpreting signs. Interestingly, fake flowers and plastic plants do not have the same effects.[12]

After Robin died, I felt extremely low, to the point that I could hardly get out of bed, but I didn't want to be totally sedentary, so I would force myself to leave the house and go for a half-hour walk in the woods around our Hampshire home every day. I knew it was good for me physically, and there wasn't much else I felt able to do, so after a few weeks I decided to go for an hour instead of half an hour, and, within a week, I could feel the difference in terms of my mental health. The physical activity had been helpful, but what really made an impact was a fuller immersion in the nature that was all around me. This time spent in nature was a form of forest bathing, and it was a major factor in me not only navigating my grief, but also welcoming signs into my life. During those walks, I would follow paths and take turnings I'd never gone down before, and I've got a terrible sense of direction, so I don't normally do that. But I felt guided and safe, as if I had been there before and nature, or something I could not explain, would point me in the right direction.

Immerse Yourself in Nature

I acknowledge that it can feel hard to incorporate nature into our modern lives because of how distant many of us are from it now, especially those of us who live in cities, but harnessing the benefits of nature does not require you to start camping out every weekend in the wilderness. There are accessible steps that you can incorporate into your everyday life that can provide you with the stress-reducing and calm-inducing benefits of nature. Here are some suggestions as to how you can re-engage with nature in positive but easy ways that will help you to notice and take advantage of signs in your life.

Try grounding

Fortunately, you don't have to travel far from home in order to experience nature. One of the best ways I have found to create a strong physical connection to the natural world, beyond simply being in it, is the act of earthing or grounding. This practice involves spending time either barefoot or without rubber-soled shoes on natural surfaces such as grass or sand. The reason you don't want rubber in your shoes is so that you are not blocking the flow of energy from the earth. You can now buy barefoot shoes, some of which have copper in them to allow electrons to flow freely from the earth to the body, which has potential health benefits, including regulating circadian rhythm, reducing inflammation, pain management, better sleep, reduced stress, more energy and blood pressure regulation.[13] You can also swim in the sea or fresh water, both of which are increasingly popular, as immersion in nature of all sorts is really good for you, and the conductive properties of the electrons in natural water also constitute a form of grounding.[14]

On my visit to the Navajo Nation in 2023, I bought a pair of moccasins that have a soft suede sole, and if I don't have the time for a long walk, I often go to my local churchyard and walk on the grass there and ground myself that way. Similarly, any time I go to a beach, I kick off my shoes immediately and walk barefoot on the sand and at least dip my toes into the water. It might seem a bit odd at first, but I highly recommend that you try grounding by taking your socks and shoes off and walking on the grass in your garden if you have one, or the next time you visit your local park.

Engage your senses

I've become something of a tree-hugger! Whenever I'm in the woods, I love to feel all of the different textures and really engage all of my senses (as we discussed in Chapter 4). If I see a leaf that looks like an interesting texture, I'll be compelled to touch it, and if I see a beautiful flower, I'll really look at the colour and shape of the petals and smell it as well. I like to grow edible flowers, such as nasturtiums or magnolia petals, to put into salads, and I go foraging for wild garlic when it's in season.

I also love to listen to all of the sounds in nature, such as waves crashing or the gentle tinkle of a stream, but especially birdsong, which is also more accessible to most of us. Julian Treasure, author of *Sound Business*, said, 'People find birdsong relaxing and reassuring because over thousands of years they have learnt when the birds sing they are safe. It's when birds stop singing that people need to worry.'[15] As I've mentioned, I particularly listen out for robins and rush to see if I can see one whenever I hear a robin's song, although I often can't. Instead, I just give thanks for the feeling of safety the sound promises. If you don't have time for a long walk, at least sit outside and listen out for birdsong and see how it makes you feel.

Fire gazing, which is something our ancestors would have done when they sat around an open fire at night, is another good way to engage your senses in a natural setting, and it has been shown to reduce blood pressure[16] and produce an anti-inflammatory reaction.[17] Early humans would also have gazed at the stars in the sky, which has been shown to promote better mental health by inducing feelings of awe and providing perspective.[18] Stargazing can be tricky if you live in a city because of the light pollution, but if you have the opportunity to look at the night sky while in the countryside or somewhere more remote, you won't be disappointed.

I encourage you to do as many things to engage your senses in nature as you can and incorporate these activities as micro-habits whenever you are able to. The idea is to experience nature fully and appreciate it in all its facets, thereby extracting even more of its benefits. Don't be afraid to get your hands dirty, both figuratively and literally.

Incorporate nature in your home

You don't even need to leave home to incorporate more nature into your life. I enjoy gardening and think very carefully about the colour schemes of my plants and flowers for each season, which has a positive effect on my mood every morning. In fact, I would go as far as to say that gardening and horticulture more generally are creative acts, which bring with them all of the benefits that we discussed in the previous chapter. However, it goes further than this. Direct contact with the earth has also been proven to be beneficial in terms of our mental well-being. In experiments on mice, contact with the bacteria *Mycobacterium vaccae*, commonly found in soil, was shown to boost serotonin and have an antidepressant-like effect.[19]

Not everyone is fortunate enough to have a garden, of course, but if you've got a balcony or a windowsill, you can still bring nature into your environment. Having plants in your home is another easy way of enhancing your physical environment on the one hand, and also the tending of them contributes to your well-being on the other. There are particular varieties, such as spider plants, peace lilies, snake plants and aloe vera, that are very good at oxygenating the atmosphere and purifying the air in your home.[20] But the tending of the plants is almost more important than what they look like or the contribution they make to your air quality. Looking after them is a mini inter-action with nature. I talk to my plants and tell them they're beautiful, and I really notice when there are new shoots and praise them. It's a very accessible way of interacting with nature. You can take cuttings from neighbours or friends, so it also doesn't need to involve a lot of expense.

Even if your access to nature is limited, looking at images or videos of nature or listening to nature sounds have been shown to have a positive impact.[21] You can have pictures of nature (birds, animals, plants, oceans, mountains and so on) and vases of cut flowers around your home, and there are radio stations that play birdsong and other nature sounds. On YouTube there are lots of videos of things such as running water, the sun moving across the sky above rugged mountain peaks and beautiful wooded landscapes. These are arguably among the most basic ways of bringing nature into your home, and they are therefore useful to a degree, but they are ultimately not as impactful as the real thing, so I wouldn't suggest that you rely on these substitutes alone.

Texture also plays a part in how we experience our environments. As a case in point, I've always loved diverse textures, and I would recommend that you try to introduce natural textures into your living environment. For example, I once bought a tile that had a geode in it because I liked the look and feel of it. I also have a number of crystals on display in my house, including two really big geodes: a purple amethyst, for peace and serenity, that's near the front doorway, and a yellow citrine, for abundance and prosperity. I've also got smaller ones on my bedside table, so that they can influence me while I'm asleep, rose quartz, which symbolises love, on my desk and a bowl in my living area with smaller crystals that people have gifted me.

When it comes to nature smells at home, you can have naturally scented candles made from plant-based waxes, such as soy or coconut, and diffusers with essential oils around your home, and I sometimes light incense sticks or cones, which is part of my cultural heritage. You could use sage or palo santo, or whatever resonates for you. You can also pick some wild flowers and introduce natural scents that way.

Limit your exposure to artificial or toxic stimuli

At the other end of the spectrum, most of us would agree that pollution is the antithesis of nature, but we would probably be shocked to know that a lack of calm, positive stimuli for our senses is bad for us as well. That's why bringing more nature into your environment also means avoiding things, where possible, that are bad for your senses, such as noise or light pollution. As well as enriching your interaction with your environment, it's about having awareness of things that can affect you and assault your senses, because that's something you can have control over to a degree.

Thinking back to Marian Diamond's experiment (page 155), it didn't surprise me at all that being in an enriched environment caused the rats' brains to grow, but I didn't think that a deprived environment would actually make them shrink. That, to me, was quite shocking. I thought a deprived environment would be the same as the neutral environment, in that it would have no effect. This demonstrates that filling your home with all sorts of natural colours, scents and textures that are right for you is really good for your brain, but the cost of not doing it is an even bigger driver.

Towards a Deeper Connection with Nature

There are lots of ways in which we can see our connection with nature: we are all part of the food chain; without plants, there would be no oxygen for us to breathe; we share genetic similarities, to a lesser or greater degree, with all living things, because we have all ultimately evolved from a common ancestor if we go back far enough; we are all made of the same organic elements; we have a symbiotic relationship with bacteria; and so on. But could it be that we are also connected with nature in ways we don't yet understand? After all, many of the signs that resonate with people come from nature in some way, whether that is birds, feathers or even the heart shapes that I often see in natural objects.

The connections revealed by science

Scientists are showing us connections within nature that we could not have dreamt of a few years ago, which could well point to the fact that there is more to be learnt about our own connection with nature in the future.

In recent years, significant advances have been made in our understanding of plant communication in particular. For example, it is now known that mycelium, which makes up the root-like structures of fungi, interacts with the roots of plants and trees to create what is known as the mycorrhizal network. This connects individual plants and trees together so that they can transfer water, nitrogen, carbon and other minerals. But even more remarkably, it also seems as though this network facilitates a form of communication. If a plant or tree detects some sort of threat in a different part of the forest, it can change its biochemistry to support the one in need.[22] When a tree is felled, other trees reach out to the stump, offering water and sugar through their root tips via the mycorrhizal network. This continuous sustenance can keep the stump alive for decades and even centuries. And they don't only do this for trees of the same species, presumably because there is a symbiotic relationship in which their lives depend on the health of the whole ecosystem. In the past, this would have been considered to be fantastical, but over the last 20 or 30 years, the science has backed up this theory.

Trees, fungi and mycelium do not have nervous systems, but they do have senses and awareness of sorts, and can make decisions, communicate with each other and perform acts of self-preservation. Mycologists compare the electrical pulses in the hyphal strands of fungi to neural networks in the human brain, and researchers are looking into using mycelium to make music, computers, a type of artificial brain, a leather substitute and even bricks.[23]

As well as communicating via mycorrhizal networks, trees can also interact with each other by secreting chemicals. For example, on safari 15 years ago, a guide told me that if giraffes overeat acacia trees, the trees secrete an airborne chemical that warns other acacia trees in the vicinity to turn bitter so the giraffes won't eat them all, and science has now confirmed this to be true.[24]

So, trees can interact with each other by secreting chemicals that can change their physiology, and mycelium interacts with trees, conveying messages between them. It also seems like plants can interact with humans too. Certain trees, such as pines, oaks, eucalyptuses, cedars, spruces and firs, emit chemicals called phytoncides that trigger the release of natural killer (NK) cells in human immune systems, boosting our ability to fight off everything from colds and flus all the way up to eliminating small cancerous cells.[25] This effect has also been shown to work outside a nature setting. One experiment demonstrated that exposure to essential oils from trees that contained phytoncides in an urban setting led to a decrease in stress hormones and an increase in NK activity.[26]

The connections revealed by ancient wisdom

Although it remains conjecture for the moment, these relationships between mycelium networks and trees, and trees and us, perhaps point to the fact that there is much more about our own interconnection with nature and all living things that is yet to be proven by science. It was certainly the case that our ancestors believed us to be inextricably linked with nature.

Even though the traditions of ancient cultures were for the most part oral in nature, and as such many practices have inevitably been lost to us, we can look to traditional cultures that still exist today for guidance and a better understanding of the belief that all living things are connected that humans once had. For instance, Australian Aboriginal and Torres Strait Islanders are the oldest living cultures in the world, and both have a deep connection to nature and the environment, considering themselves to be part of the natural world and to have a responsibility to care for it. They know how to use and conserve natural resources for food, medicine, shelter and tools, and how the seasons affect plants and animals. They have developed sustainable practices such as firestick farming, which is still used today, and Dadirri, which involves deep inner listening and awareness and is at least 40,000 years old. They also use totems to symbolise the connections between people, the physical world and spiritual powers. When I lived in Darwin, white cockatoos were an extremely common sight, and I used to think it was funny that they were like the pigeons of London but so much more beautiful. The Aboriginal liaison officer I worked with told me that the rarer black cockatoos are believed to be their deceased ancestors in animal form, and they consider it extremely auspicious to see them.

Across the Tasman Sea, *Te Ao Māori* is the holistic world view of the Māori people of New Zealand that emphasises the interconnection of people and nature. *Ko ahau te taiao, ko te taiao ko ahau* ('I am the environment, and the environment is me') is a phrase that demonstrates the relationship between the health of the ecosystem and the well-being of the people, while *whakapapa* describes the connection between people, the landscape and plants and animals, and how they came into being. The Māori people consider themselves guardians of the natural world, responsible for preserving the life force, sacred sites and treasures such as land, soil and water. They believe that everything living and non-living is interconnected and that humans are descendants of the sky father. They also believe in a spiritual connection to the earth mother who sustains all life.

The ancient Hindu Vedic texts teach that nature is the manifestation of the Divine Mother, and that nature cannot be destroyed without humans being destroyed. They also say that humans are part of nature and should love and respect it.

Another good example is the First Americans, who have a long-standing relationship with nature. Their teachings emphasise a close connection between humans and the natural world; indeed, that humans are part of nature and not separate from it and that everything is connected in a symbiotic cycle. They believe that everything in nature has a spirit, including plants, animals, rocks, rivers and humans, and that humans should work with these spirits rather than trying to control them. They pray before taking anything from the land, and the sun dance is a ceremony that honours all life and its source.

When I interviewed him, Bird Runningwater, a member of the Cheyenne and Mescalero Apache Tribal Nations and the director of the Sundance Institute's Native American and Indigenous programme for 20 years, said that one of the ways that First American culture was damaged by colonialism was by breaking this deep connection with nature, particularly by taking away the foods that they were naturally used to eating. So, the extermination of the bison and the replacement of corn with rice were actually means of undermining the way of life of the First Americans.

Because so many cultures around the world believed this interconnection between people and nature to be fundamental to existence, I sometimes wonder if we have in effect done something akin to what colonisation did to the First Americans to ourselves in the modern world by breaking our bond with nature. If that is the case, it would make sense that we are less able to access our signs, as we would not be gaining all of the benefits that our interconnection with nature has to offer.

It's not just that these cultures believe in an interconnectedness; they also seem to be able to harness a connection with nature in ways we can barely imagine in the Western world. This can be seen in the ability of traditional cultures to read the land today. In the Andaman Islands, an archipelago in the Indian Ocean, there are indigenous people such as the Onge tribe who never interact with other humans and live as their ancient ancestors once did. When the Boxing Day tsunami struck in 2004, the islands were hit particularly badly, and more people died than survived, a fact that hit me really hard, as I had enjoyed my first honeymoon there. However, among the indigenous tribes, there were very few casualties. It is believed that their deep-rooted understanding of their environment and knowledge passed down via their oral traditions told them to retreat to higher ground.[27] It is also possible that they observed changes in the behaviour of birds and aquatic life, as there is some speculation that animals can detect earthquakes in advance. It is very difficult to substantiate this, although efforts are now being made to track the behaviour of animals from space in order to help predict the occurrence of natural disasters.[28]

But what is it that allows traditional people to harness their connection with nature in ways like this? Bird Runningwater suggested a reason for this when I asked him why their land is so important to him and his people, and why they couldn't just make a new place their own once they had been displaced. He said that the rock formations and types of trees, the animals that naturally roam there and the foods that normally grow there create a connection to that specific landscape for his people. It's not the same to be just anywhere else, even if it looks nice or seems to provide for your needs. And the connections that they forge with that particular place allow them to read the wide range of signs that nature provides more accurately, whether that be something material like the weather and stars, or something spiritual such as their communication with ancestors.

All of these examples point to the fact that ancient people, and people more in tune with nature than most of us are today, have access to information from the natural environment that we have lost sight of, distracted as we are by scientific and technological progress.

Of course, this speaks to a practical understanding of their surroundings; however, many traditional cultures also believe there is a spiritual aspect to this knowledge – for instance, that it is their ancestors or deities looking out for them. This is perhaps because they are relying on their intuition rather than their intellect to interpret what the natural world is telling them and therefore seeing a spiritual explanation for their connection to and understanding of nature. To the Onge tribe, cloud formations could on the one hand be a sign of rain coming, but on the other a sign that someone is looking down on them and protecting or guiding them.

The use of psychedelics

Many indigenous and ancient cultures relied on signs from beyond to guide them and give meaning to their lives. And one of the ways in which some cultures accessed the spiritual realm was via the use of psychedelics (a term that literally means 'mind manifesting'), as these substances often provoke a strong sense of oneness and a feeling of interconnection between all living things.

To fully understand why psychedelics were held in high regard and used in ceremonies requires an understanding of the very different belief systems ancient and traditional people had and have for interacting with and interpreting the world around them – ideologies that I believe we have much to learn from, especially if we can look at why they did what they did and not just emulate their practices mindlessly. For example, we've seen that most traditional cultures don't have a sense of division between what is human and what is natural in the way that many of us do. Our prioritisation of our cognitive, conscious minds has led to us creating this sense of separation. Over the years, some westernised people have attempted to break down this perceived barrier by taking psychedelics. However, that's the wrong way of thinking, because the ancient and indigenous cultures that have taken psychedelic substances over the years already believe they're one and the same as nature and the universe, and they instead take psychedelics to expand their experience of life. It would confound them if you suggested that we were in some way separate from nature.

Some ancient people called these substances 'spirit medicines', and they have played a large role in many cultures and religions. To name but a few, the Native American Church in the USA, which combines elements of indigenous beliefs with aspects of Christianity, uses peyote or the San Pedro cactus to loosen the veil between heaven and earth; Ancient Greeks used a drink called kykeon; in the Hindu Vedic tradition a concoction called soma, thought to contain cannabis, magic mushrooms or possibly ephedra, was consumed during rituals and is referred to as haoma in Zoroastrianism; in Algeria and various parts of South America they used psilocybin found in magic mushrooms as long ago as 5,000 BCE; *Amanita muscaria* (muscimol) was used as a tea by the Ancient Romans and is believed to have helped the early Christians survive persecution; and Latin American shamans consumed ayahuasca in ceremonies. These various substances were woven into early healing practices and were used to induce ASC in cultural and religious rituals, to facilitate communication with their ancestors and to access other realms of being. These practices were also undertaken to help people gain information about the world around them and expand their consciousness more generally, so that they were more in tune with the signs in everyday life too.

Modern neuroscience provides us with an explanation of what is going on in the brain when humans ingest psychedelics. We now know that these substances act on 5-HT_{2A} receptors that regulate brain function. The human brain has the highest 5-HT_{2A} receptor density of any animal, with particularly high densities in the neocortex, the most recently evolved part of the brain.[29] As these receptors are stimulated, for example by the psychedelic drug LSD, they increase emotional impact and the sense of awe and wonder, and improve integration (interconnectedness) across the brain, especially heightened visual connectivity, hence the complex hallucinations often associated with psychedelics.[30] Psilocybin also increases brain connectivity, which is why it can sometimes provide new solutions to old problems.[31]

But you don't need to take the risks associated with such substances to gain new perspectives on life. It may be possible to open your mind to realms beyond this physical world, as many ancient people believed, through natural means, such as via holotropic or conscious-connected breathwork (see box below), mindfulness, time in nature, creativity and somatic work. And if there is some truth to the fact that all living things are connected, techniques such as these could potentially help you to open your mind to perceiving and interpreting signs from beyond.

Holotropic breathwork

Jamie Clements, breathwork practitioner, specialises in breathing techniques to achieve ASC. He explained to me that breathwork creates a powerful vehicle for healing by providing an accessible route into transformation through ASC. Conscious-connected breathing is a technique involving a continuous circular pattern of high ventilation to create hypocapnic (low carbon dioxide) and hypoxic (low oxygen) conditions that open up a mystical experience that research has shown to be on par with medium to high doses of psilocybin.[32] Holotropic breathwork is one of the original Western schools of therapeutic breathwork, created by Stanislav and Christina Grof, who sought to find non-drug means for ASC after LSD was outlawed in the late 1960s.

Conscious-connected breathing should only be practised with a trained professional, but there are many other resources available on the app The Breath Space that I highly recommend. Kriya yoga, kriya breathing, kundalini yoga and certain meditation techniques can also induce ASC, which are characterised by shifts in perception, thoughts and emotions, sometimes leading to feelings of interconnectedness, bliss or oneness.

Although I have always been someone who would have said that spending time in nature makes you feel good, I would never have hugged a tree until quite recently. The scientist in me has made me quite sceptical at points in my life, and I would have looked for evidence before trying something. However, in recent years, as my interest in spirituality has increased, I've been more willing to lean into my intuition and do something simply because it feels right, as there are benefits of that for the brain.

For instance, it induces the feeling of harmony and alignment that is so crucial to our sense of well-being and self-trust. Yes, science is telling us that being around trees is good for our immune systems and mental health, but you don't necessarily need to have a scientific reason to touch a tree or walk barefoot on the beach. If you listen to your body, and it is telling you that something feels good, then it is probably doing you some good.

A sense of psychological safety is one of the by-products of creative practice, and there's a similar psychological safety or comfort or confidence in yourself that you get from a closer connection with nature, because it's truer to how we should be living our lives and speaks more to the essence of what it is to be human. Having a strong connection to nature makes us more in tune with things, and I think that leads to us feeling more like we can trust ourselves.

As I've said, our ancestors relied on their senses to understand their environment and their tribe. Being disconnected from nature means that we are less able to access our intuition. So, in some ways, we're blocked by modern life, because we've lost our connection with nature. If we can reharness this connection with nature that ancient cultures had, I believe that there's no reason why we can't also open our minds and better facilitate the manifestation of signs.

Nature is integral to our well-being and an important way in which we can tap into our signs more effectively. However, we mostly don't realise the impact our environments have on us, and we have become disconnected from nature – our original habitat and primary environment for millennia. Ancient cultures and ancestors had that intrinsic interconnection, and we can therefore look to them for inspiration. They demonstrate that we are actually an inseparable part of nature, and it's our cognitive minds that create this sense of separation. They also point to the possibility that we can harness this interconnection in order to access signs to help comfort and guide us. There are, therefore, real advantages to reconnecting with nature, including to our health and well-being, and also by helping us to live more in tune with our true essence and creating the best conditions to bring the transformative benefits of signs into our lives.

That just leaves us with one other area of our lives to think about when it comes to encouraging signs into our lives: our relationships with the people around us.

KEY TAKEAWAYS

1. We are part of nature, and this is ancient wisdom we have forgotten.
2. Time in nature has immune-boosting and longevity benefits for humans.
3. Nature is a source of many of our signs.

CHAPTER 8

CONNECT WITH EACH OTHER

T wo months after I moved back to London, I went to stay with Alfie, Robin's friend of 30 years and someone who had become a great support to me after Robin passed. He lives five minutes away from our old house in Hampshire, so when I was there, I told him I wanted to go and see the tree that's planted in the church across the road from where we lived, because there's a small plaque there for Robin. I chose a maple tree because Robin fondly remembered drinking maple syrup straight from the source when he was growing up.

After the visit, when we got back in the car and turned on the ignition, there was a song playing on the radio. Alfie whipped his head round and looked at me, but I did not understand the significance until he said, 'It's a Justin Bieber song.' Alfie is not someone who would usually put much value on something he saw as paranormal, but this song playing at this moment was meaningful for him – and for me – because Bieber was Robin's surname too. We were both thinking deeply about Robin in that moment, and, as I've mentioned, I believe that strong emotions open the way for signs from lost loved ones. The lyrics were also particularly meaningful for me as we drove past the home where we had been so happy. In a situation such as this, having a shared experience with someone to support me was vital to me being able to see my signs more clearly and not feel like I was distorting the importance of them.

I believe that in the Western world we've underestimated the importance of our connection to each other. How we are living today is a far cry from the ways we lived for thousands of years of our evolution. Our influence on each other is unavoidable, real and measurable. If you optimise those influences, and reap the benefits of an aligned and supportive tribe, there are intrinsic benefits to your health and well-being. In a paper in the *Journal of Medical Ethics and History of Medicine* that describes the dimensions, components and indicators of spiritual health, it includes human connection with others. They write that the participants in the study believed that a connection with others could positively affect an individual's behaviour and result in acceptance of social responsibility, respect for the rights of others, honesty, compassion, altruism, generosity, optimism, empathy, benevolence, helping others unconditionally, humility and lack of jealousy or grudge-keeping.[1] A strong connection with others is also another major contributing factor in creating the conditions for you to receive and interpret signs, because it provides the psychological safety and faith to trust the signs that you receive or to discuss their interpretation should you need to. Because our signs are in large part a consequence of our spiritual connections to each other, if we isolate ourselves, we are limiting our ability to access them. In other words, our signs are stronger and more abundant if we have better connections with others.

Our Need for Each Other

I believe that there is a strong need in each of us to forge close connections with others, an urge that I'm sure most people would recognise in themselves to one degree or another. This need for connection again goes back to the earliest days of humanity. Being part of a tribe is our most natural mode of being and a fundamental feature of our evolutionary psychology. When early humans lived in caves during the Palaeolithic era, or Stone Age, and it was cold overnight, they had to huddle together for warmth and to avoid predation.[2] Individuals would band together in groups of no more than a few dozen, depending on the available resources,[3] and their survival would be closely linked to that of everyone else. To this end, everyone would have a purpose, such as hunting, gathering, taking care of the cave environment, meal preparation and reproduction, even if that meant individuals sacrificing for the greater good. Early humans also realised that you had to create emotional warmth in the tribe to keep it together. This need was embodied by sitting around the campfire in the evening and drumming or dancing and by the other bonding activities they undertook, such as storytelling through art or adorning each other, and shared care of the children.

Having evolved in this way, we have a deep desire to have meaningful connections, and we require this from a wider network than just a nuclear family. We need to deliberately seek that out today, with many of us in Western society becoming much more isolated, particularly from our wider communities, such as neighbours, local retailers and religious groups. We tend to prioritise ourselves, our immediate family, a handful of friends and our work colleagues. This is problematic, because feelings of loneliness are widespread. According to a worldwide survey of people from 142 countries conducted by Gallup, almost a quarter of all adults feel 'very' or 'fairly' lonely, with higher levels among young people than older people, suggesting that loneliness is on the rise.[4] And studies have shown that being lonely decreases life expectancy and can be as bad for your health as smoking.[5] Social isolation has also been linked to depression and the shrinking of the memory centres of the brain (reducing grey matter volume in the hippocampus). Living together in ways that foster community, belonging and connection with others is therefore essential for cognitive well-being.[6]

Although we no longer need to rely on the direct contribution of those around us for survival, none of us are an island unto ourselves. We feel the benefits of the care of others, and we also benefit from having something to offer. A need to be in service to other people is intrinsic to our existence – we all need a purpose that transcends ourselves.

Unfortunately, in a modern world defined by individualism, with remote working, urbanisation, online and social media interactions often being prioritised over face-to-face interactions, and dating apps that allow us to treat people as disposable, many of us have lost our deep connection with others, especially in the Western world. As we have moved to a society in which the individual is prioritised above the collective, we have undermined the fact that we are social creatures who flourish best when part of a tribe. But not only do we sacrifice loving support if we do not have people to lean on, not to mention missing out on the benefits of performing acts of service and kindness for our tribe, we are also doing ourselves a disservice because our minds cannot be at their best without them, and we are not, therefore, creating the optimum conditions for us to welcome signs into our lives. This is why it is so important that we reprioritise our tribes.

Our unconscious influence over each other

Having evolved to be part of a tribe, our bodies have developed interesting responses to the people around us; for example, we receive information from things like body language and facial expressions, including micro-muscular changes. Some of these signals are registered consciously, but many of them are non-conscious processes that have an impact on our brains and bodies without us realising. Often non-verbal cues, such as how much eye contact you make and your tone of voice, speak the loudest. And the people around us can also have a strong impact on us psychologically, which can lead to us behaving in ways that are not to our benefit – for instance, we can be influenced by social contagion, whereby certain trends such as divorce or doping among athletes become normalised and have a domino effect on the people within that group.

This deep connection with other people is not just at the psychological level – we are also constantly sending information to and receiving it from other people (some of it chemical) in ways that we are not always conscious of. For example, although the research has yet to find a causal link, many people believe that we are affected by the people immediately around us via the airborne transfer of hormones such as cortisol, which leak out via our sweat. This would work by the particles that linger in the air being absorbed by us and then impacting our own stress levels. What has been proven is that just witnessing someone who is stressed raises our own cortisol levels, even if we are not directly exposed to or aware of what the stressor is.[7] We can also be affected hormonally by the love expressed by others. For example, oxytocin is released by hugging, kissing, sex and looking at cute baby animals such as large-eyed puppies.

Our sense of smell is one of the major ways that we bond and build strong emotional connections. For instance, when you enter your parents' or grandparents' houses, you get an avalanche of memories, because those smells are connected to all your childhood memories. Some research suggests that smell also plays a function in how we choose our romantic partners via the major histocompatibility complex, which is the basis of our adaptive immune system.[8] The theory is that it benefits future children to have a 'bilingual' immune system, so some people believe that we might be attracted to an immune system that is as different as possible from our own. This would be a means to ensure the effective creation of offspring, rather than a predictor of the success of the relationship.

There is a non-conscious chemical element to the way we bond with other people in a romantic context. Some of the research on this has been done on voles, because meadow and mountain voles are promiscuous, but prairie and pine voles are monogamous, which is rare in mammals. The latter will share a nest, defend their territory, raise young together, work for access to their mate, have empathy when their mate is stressed, console each other via touch and always prefer their mate to the choice of a stranger. This is due to the sparsity of food and shelter – it makes more sense for the male to settle down with one mate and defend the home rather than pursue multiple females. In this way, the female gets help with childcare and protection against intruders. The hormones oxytocin and vasopressin are crucial to this behaviour, as they help to promote the monogamous behaviour in the males, and researchers have discovered that there are extra receptors for these hormones in the brains of prairie and pine voles that meadow and mountain voles do not have. Neurons in the nucleus accumbens and ventral pallidum, the reward pathways of the brain, fire when the mate is close, and the number of neurons increases as the bond deepens. Additionally, when more genes for oxytocin and vasopressin get switched on, the promiscuous voles prefer cuddling to sex, shifting from promiscuous to monogamous behaviour. Sexual activity also drives the wiring. The voles' brains are primed for certain default social behaviours, but repeated sexual activity switches on genes for learning and memory (possibly also mediated via smell), as well as genes in the reward circuit, making them want to stay bonded to the same partner.[9] This hormonal process plays out in humans too. For example, seeing a picture of or holding the hands of loved ones leads to increased blood flow to the nucleus accumbens, deepening existing bonds.

The hormone vasopressin plays a part in blood pressure regulation, blood osmolality (electrolyte balance) and blood volume, and it is crucial to how men form relationships, because it also influences social behaviour and bonding and regulates aggression (guarding a partner or territory). Waiting to have sex increases vasopressin in men, as it increases during arousal but drops after sex, reducing the likelihood of bonding. For women, dopamine and oxytocin will increase if they are enjoying dating and are sexually interested. For men, dopamine, vasopressin and testosterone increases lead to the guarding, protective and possessive behaviours more likely to result in the sustaining of a relationship long term.

These hormonal responses are triggered by the behaviours of our prospective mates, but we do not realise how much they can influence our decision-making. However, if you are aware that these processes are happening, you can use this knowledge to inform how you select a partner. For example, if you are a woman, waiting to have sex during the early stages of courtship might allow you the time to judge whether your prospective partner is really interested in a long-term relationship rather than being unduly influenced by the build-up of vasopressin while they hope for sex, and give you the space to spot any other red flags. It is also likely that a man who is only exhibiting bonding signals because of vasopressin will lose interest if their desire for sex is not soon fulfilled.

Although research in this field tends to focus primarily on opposite-sex couples, studies have been done that show there are similarities in brain structure between straight men and gay women, and between gay men and straight women, which perhaps hints at the fact that some of the same hormonal responses could be playing out in gay relationships.[10] However, more research clearly needs to be done on this.

This is why it is helpful to be aware of the physical signals and hormonal interactions that guide our decision-making for romance. If we make a bad choice or have a break-up, it will affect our cognition and reduce our self-trust, dampening our ability to notice signs. We often don't see the things that we don't want to, but, in retrospect, there were usually flags that a relationship was ending or not going in the right direction from the start. If we can regulate our emotions, understand the impact of our hormones and follow guidance from our signs, we are much more likely to get a good long-term outcome and bolster our trust in ourselves.

Curating Your Tribe

In a society that puts so much value on the individual, some of us might have lost sight of what our tribe is. British anthropologist Robin Dunbar argues that our personal social network is limited to approximately 150 people on average, based on the cognitive limit of how many people we can maintain stable relationships with.[11] This network consists of our romantic partners, immediate family members, friends, work colleagues and acquaintances. These are the personalities with whom we interact most often, and who can therefore have the most profound impact on us.

Because there are so many ways in which this network can influence us, directly and indirectly, I believe we should curate our tribes very mindfully. It is not about dumping friendships or relationships unkindly, but where values don't align, relationships do tend to gently drift apart, and this doesn't always have to be seen as a form of rejection or abandonment. We can wish the other person well even if we are on different journeys. So, try to notice who leaves you feeling drained and unsupported versus who makes you feel calm or energised when you need it.

I think it's also healthy to try to meet new people, get to know them and, where values really align, nurture the mutual benefits to build new friendships. Much like neural networks in the brain, in which connections are strengthened or pruned, we need to think carefully about our personal community and how we are each contributing, so we can understand where to direct energy into strengthening supportive connections.

Beyond our personal networks, we are also influenced by our wider communities, which are made up of the people who live in the same place as us and groups of people with whom we share common interests or beliefs. How we treat these people is just as important to us and our well-being as how we treat those in our immediate families and friendship groups. It doesn't really cost you anything to smile at someone, and it makes a difference on a personal level, and also potentially on a community level too. You're not necessarily closely bonding with someone who you buy your coffee from if you smile at them, but some researchers argue that when the fabric of society breaks down – for example, during riots – oxytocin levels are lower than normal, which leads to lower levels of trust.[12] Small moments of kindness help to marginally increase oxytocin. If this effect was replicated across communities, it would have a subtle but profound impact on social cohesion.

When it comes to being kind to people and connecting with strangers, I always think of the last scene from the film *About Time*. The protagonist is able to time travel, and he begins by repeatedly going back to scenarios in the past to tweak them so that he can attain his dream life. However, in the end he realises that living in the present moment and really savouring what he has is a bigger gift, so instead of rushing through his day and grabbing his coffee from the server and jumping on the train, he takes a second to pause and make eye contact with the person and smile and say good morning, even though he doesn't know them and might never see them again. These small moments of kindness add up to provide us with the overall feeling of connection and subsequent well-being that we're all seeking in our lives.

Going that small extra step with everyone you interact with is going to increase your oxytocin levels, just as gratitude and appreciating beauty do, and in that state you're more likely to receive signs, because oxytocin correlates to emotions such as joy, excitement, love and trust, which help you to lower your guard and be more open. It's also going to boost your ability to notice the people and the world around you, which will help you to observe things more generally, because you're in an open, relaxed, stress-free frame of mind.

Society at large can also have a big impact on you. You might not directly interact with the overwhelming majority of people who make up the society in which you live, but it is impossible to escape the influence of people at a collective level. Popular culture and the zeitgeist, politics, and older and younger generations are just some of the societal-level groupings or influences that inform our understanding of our place in the world. And a feeling of togetherness and connection, even on this grander scale, is therefore conducive to living a life with signs.

Feeling connected to contemporary culture is a good way to forge a sense of connection. It may seem inconsequential on the face of it, but just think about how it makes you feel if all of your friends are talking about the latest hit TV programme but you've not watched it yet. It can be quite isolating to feel separated from the things that help to bind us together. Of course, there is no such thing as one overarching culture that we all need to tap into – culture is diverse and means different things to different people. The important thing is to feel part of a culture that speaks to you and then interact with it in a meaningful way.

Values are what draw us together in our communities, so we also need to be really clear on what our own values are and who we want to align them with. Asking yourself what you are naturally drawn to and passionate about and making sure that's present in your life is going to give you a greater sense of fulfilment. A simple way to do this is to think of a character trait in other people that you particularly dislike – the opposite of this is likely to be extremely important to you. So, for example, if you really don't like it when people are selfish, generosity is probably one of your core values. This alignment of values creates another layer of harmony that brings and keeps the right people in your life and better lends itself to you noticing signs.

Be the kind of friend you want

When people are looking for a partner, they usually focus on what they want in the other person. The same applies when you are trying to meet new friends. Instead, make a list of what you are looking for in the people around you and then ask yourself if you are all of those things, because if you're not, you're less likely to be able to attract those sorts of people. Be the person who is the kind of friend you want, as it is then much more likely that those sorts of people will come into your life. It's again about being proactive and not completely reactive to the people around you and putting out something positive into the world.

Being aware of how your cultural heritage is feeding into your sense of identity within your tribe is also worthwhile. On a business trip to Singapore, I paid a visit to the Asian Civilisations Museum, which is an amazingly curated museum. While I was there, I realised that they were describing Asian cultures using the word 'we', whereas if I go to the British Museum and visit the Asian section, the descriptions alongside the artefacts use the word 'they'. I'd never before thought about how that made me feel like I was 'other'. Being of Asian heritage, the simple use of the word 'we' made me feel a sense of pride and emotional connection that I had not felt in a museum before, because in the past I had just been read-ing historical facts detached from my direct experience, and they only affected my logical brain. Reconnecting with your cultural heritage, whether it be through food, music, art or community, especially for oppressed or marginalised groups, can also be very beneficial for improving your sense of 'self' and finding meaning and a sense of community.

We can also look to ancient cultures and how they foster this connection to their ancestors for guidance. Traditions that are passed down the generations create a sense of fraternity with the people who share those traditions on a societal level, and also, importantly, with the people who came before you. First Americans, the Nigerian Yoruba tribe and many other indigenous cultures are very connected to their ancestors via their traditions, and connecting with and revering their ances-tors is an intrinsic part of their day-to-day life in a way that we don't experience so much any more. I was brought up like this; for example, my mother would leave food offerings for our ancestors. In ancient cultures such as Hinduism and Jainism, it is believed that ancestors, lost loved ones or other benevo-lent entities such as deities or angels can exert influence in our world, such as by changing the weather or sending us signs often connected to nature.

I know it's not always easy to find meaningful relationships if they are absent in your life. However, it is an essential part of who we are, so I want to empower you to seek out ways to find your tribe if you do not have one at the moment, because there are things that you can do to find a sense of community, or a friendship, or an interaction that is nurturing. To summarise, these include:

- engaging in small acts of kindness
- interacting with contemporary culture

- identifying your core values and aligning yourself with like-minded people

- reconnecting with your cultural heritage

- forging a connection with your ancestors and asking them to send you signs

Invoke past mentors

One practical exercise you can do to help you feel more connected to the people who came before you is the 'Mentors across Time' exercise. When I went to Brazil to do my first TEDx talk, I was nervous, as I was discussing a totally new topic, and I was performing it live in front of an audience and being filmed. The organiser took me to a Buddhist temple on the edge of town the day before and asked me to imagine all the teachers who had come before me standing behind me across time and supporting me with their knowledge and skills. It was a powerful visual that I believe helped me a lot, and it is very simple to do:

1. Decide who you want support from, whether that is your own ancestors, people who came before you in the industry you are in, or any other kind of tribe.

2. Close your eyes and visualise all the mentors across time that have come before you and imagine them all standing behind you.

3. Notice what it feels like to have that support.

4. Ask yourself what they might say to you and pay attention to their facial expressions and body language.

5. Feel your energy being filled up by their loving support and reassurance.

6. After you've opened your eyes, journal about the
   experience.

Tapping into the Collective Unconscious

These different layers of personal and communal interaction
point to the fact that we are intrinsically social creatures, and
that we are all connected mentally, emotionally and spiritually. This connection is with the people physically alive today,
but what if it was also possible to maintain a connection with
people who have died and/or a universal power or source of
consciousness that includes other benevolent spirits or ancestors? As we saw in Chapter 1, the immortality of the soul has
been discussed for millennia, from the Greek philosophers
Aristotle, Plato and Socrates to the most ancient Vedic texts of
South Asia, and modern science has not yet answered the hard
question of consciousness, leaving the door open for us to widen
our network of support and guidance beyond the people present
in our lives today.

One way to think about this potential spiritual connection
is Carl Jung's theory of the collective unconscious (as opposed
to the 'personal unconscious', which is informed by our own
experiences, and the 'collective consciousness', which Jung
equated with consensus reality, or the prevailing ideologies of
the age), because it creates a point of psychological commonality between all people. Jung believed that all humanity shares
unconscious mental concepts that are derived from universal
psychological experiences stemming from ancestral experience
and inherited brain structure. Although studies have shown that
we can inherit mental health conditions, and that these conditions can be linked to variations in brain structure and function,
the underlying neural mechanisms are not yet clear, and the
same is true of Jung's universal mental concepts.[13] However,

according to Jung's theory, these shared experiences from across time – namely birth, life and death, which are things we all experience and have since time began – remain present in the unconscious and cannot be explained by things we have personally experienced. Jung coined archetypes to help us understand these fundamental shared concepts, experiences or instincts – for example, the wise old man, the crone, the warrior and the rebel – and these archetypes, with their shared values and commonalities, can be seen throughout many different cultures and civilisations.

There are minimal and maximal interpretations of Jung's theory. The minimal interpretation is based on the idea that a common genetic inheritance in terms of our brain structure leads to similarities in the way that our unconscious works. And the maximal interpretation is that there's some sort of power, world mind or universal consciousness that is the source of these shared archetypes. My experience and research by people such as Dr Greyson (who we met on page 21) suggest to me that there is something to the maximal interpretation, as I believe more and more that there is a 'cosmic force', or some sort of shared consciousness, or godhead, or the universe, or angels, or whatever label is meaningful and makes sense to you, that we can access in order to receive the signs that we need to guide us. Personally, I believe that most of my signs and messages are from Robin, and that some are from other lost loved ones, and that perhaps they have become angels. And I believe that the mechanism through which this is possible is a cosmic force made up of the consciousness of every soul.

If, when someone dies, their consciousness goes into that collective, and you can tap into it, then you could get broader guidance and protection from all the wisdom in that cosmic force, and also, potentially, from your lost loved ones directly. Some of the things that could put you in the best place to potentially tap into this cosmic force include the practices described in previous chapters; for example, meditation, certain types of breathwork, spending time in nature and creative activities. But I believe signs are the main way we can access this amazing source of knowledge and wisdom, allowing us a window into the universal consciousness.

Even simply having conversations with friends about things like this could possibly help you to tap into this higher power. Talking about signs can give the people you know comfort that it's okay to share their own experiences, and it can even bring new people into your life who have similar stories, as it has for me. As I discussed earlier in the book, I have often found that when I talk about it with people who I might not expect would be open to the idea of signs, they in fact have their own stories of sensing a presence or feeling connected to or being guided by lost loved ones. This has given me the courage to feel more comfortable to start these sorts of conversations, and this feeling of psychological safety further contributes to me feeling as though I am open to receiving signs that cannot be explained but are nonetheless beneficial to me. I want you too to feel as though you have permission and confidence to explore this aspect of life. Shared vulnerability helps people to bond, so talking about signs has also deepened many of my friendships and brought new people in, creating a virtuous circle.

Having a tribe of like-minded people who help me to have faith in my signs has been so protective during my grief in particular. For example, when Robin appeared by the side of my bed six weeks after he had passed on, the people in my tribe believed me without hesitation, thereby validating my experience. That changed my whole approach to signs, because I was a bit nervous about telling people at first. I was worried that they would think it was all just the desperation of my grief, but the fact that I have enough people around me who are willing to have that conversation and are open to things that are beyond current explanation helps me to live my life like this. And I fear that people who don't have that could end up feeling quite lost and isolated.

The crux of the matter is that you need to create the right psychological frame of mind to take advantage of signs. A generosity of spirit and a sense of openness are what you should be aiming for. If you feel like life is unfair, and this is making you inward-looking or narrow-focused, then you're less likely to be able to receive the signs that might be beneficial to you. Faith is built on optimism, hope and positivity, not pessimism, negativity or burying your head in the sand. And having even just a handful of good people around you in your community is much more likely to put you in that state of mind.

As I've said, I have increasingly come to believe in the possibility that our lost loved ones can remain part of our tribes, and that they and the universe, cosmic force, God, or whatever you want to call it, are sending us signs all the time, and we are all capable of receiving them. It's up to us whether we notice them or not. How we then interpret them, and the actions we take based on those interpretations, have the ability to transform the way we lead our lives, enriching them in immeasurable ways.

As we have seen, the connections between us are not always easily explained. Before we finish the chapter, I want to share a remarkable story that I feel demonstrates the deep connections we hold with each other and how little we understand them. Dr Mark Orpen-Lyall has a PhD in organisational psychology, specialising in resilience, and works with asset management companies. This is the story he told me of receiving signs:

I have led a charmed life, punctuated by some truly memorable moments. One of the first, witnessed by my mother, aunt and grandmother, happened during my first year. Being the son of a single mum – I only met my biological father when I was 18 – my grandfather became my 'grand father'. We had an undeniable bond.

When I was an infant, my grandfather was travelling back from KwaZulu-Natal to be with us. On a treacherous pass, a negligent driver decided to overtake on a blind rise and crashed head-on into my beloved grandfather's car. He narrowly avoided death and was rushed to the emergency room. Meanwhile, more than a thousand kilometres away, my grandmother was holding my lifeless body. I had gone a morbid blue and was slipping in and out of consciousness. Just as they were about to rush me to the emergency room, I made an inexplicable recovery.

Later that day, my grandmother got a call to say that her husband was in hospital due to a horrific car accident. She pieced together an incredible timeline. While I was 'slipping away', my grandfather was being rushed to the hospital. Luckily, my grandfather made a full recovery, and so began 12 more wonderful years with him.

Aged 69, he had heart surgery and sadly did not survive. Walking into our home on the day of his surgery, before seeing anyone, I instinctively knew that he had died. Later that day, a robin visited me and sat intently on the ledge, which I could barely see through the tears that were streaming down my face. It stayed for a long while, my companion in grief. Since that day, robins have often been there for me when I am struggling with a significant issue or when I feel most alone. I cannot explain it – they just appear, reminding me I am not alone, and that my grandfather is there watching over me. It is a bittersweet emotion. I miss him so much, but at the same time I feel so comforted that he is there.

As a practising psychologist with a PhD, I set great value in evidence-based science. But I have also come to appreciate the unexplainable, not just the provable. Just because experiences are beyond our current levels of scientific comprehension or explanation does not mean we can discount their reality. They can exist – we just do not know how.

After Mark had shared the whole story with me, I said, 'Guess what my husband's name was?' And his wife immediately replied, 'Robin.' It was a very emotional moment for all of us.

We saw in previous chapters that if you're under stress, your brain is less able to notice and interpret signs. So, if you've got people around you who drain you, then that's diminishing your mental resources, and you will be less likely to be open and able to receive signs. Furthermore, if you talk about your experience of receiving signs and people ridicule you, or just don't get it, or think it's untrue, that's also going to affect how open you are, both in terms of how willing you are to share your experiences and in terms of eventually eroding your own faith in the power of signs in your life.

In order to be able to notice signs, you have to be open to receiving them. There's a possibility that if you are being negatively influenced by people, perhaps non-consciously, it could create a kind of bias against the possibility of signs being useful to you. And this is a real threat, as we have seen in this chapter that we are influenced by other people a lot more then we realise.

The more stable and supported you are, the more likely you are to have the resources to bring signs into your life. And if you are open-minded about the possibility of some sort of shared consciousness, then feeling your connection to others and support from your tribe gets you a step closer to tapping into that wisdom. In my experience, that's when signs will become an everyday part of your life.

KEY TAKEAWAYS

1. Strong, positive and meaningful relationships bring psychological safety and a sense of belonging and purpose.
2. Our communities impact us in multiple ways, for better and worse.
3. We are connected in more ways than we realise, and this opens us up to signs.

Conclusion

On Valentine's Day 2025, one of my friends took me out for lunch and a walk, and then I had a good meeting with my colleague Simon in the afternoon. In the taxi on the way home that evening, even though I'd had a lovely day, I suddenly felt really sad that I was returning to an empty house, and I said in my head, 'Darling, you've got to send me a sign for Valentine's Day.' Soon afterwards, I heard a sports car coming up from behind. Robin loved cars, so much so that we used to drive to France and Italy every summer. The car drove past, and I noticed that it was red. I thought, 'He didn't like red sports cars, but I guess for Valentine's Day, it's appropriate.'

All of a sudden, I had an overwhelming urge that I needed to see the licence plate of that car – the sense of urgency telling me that a sign was imminent – as I felt so strongly it was going to have 'RB' in it. Sure enough, when we finally caught up with it at the next traffic lights, I could see that it was 'C21 RBN', so I took a photo of it. At that point, 'C21' didn't make any sense to me, so I googled it when I got home, but nothing relevant came up. I then texted my chief of staff, Tracie, who is also a close friend, and said, 'Something's just happened. I'm going to send you a photo.' As I was sending it, I suddenly realised what 'C21' was. Before I could tell her, Tracie responded, '"RBN" is phonetically "Robin", so it's even stronger than just "RB". And wasn't his place and date of birth Canada and 21 September?' She then texted, 'You've had so many signs, but this is the biggest one yet. I would be shaking. You probably are.'

199

This happened towards the end of me writing this book and really emphasised to me the power of the unmistakeable signs I now receive, and how integral they are to my life and work. And even though I've received so many signs now, it still takes my breath away every time it happens. It is this very special feeling of guidance and protection that I believe you can experience too.

In several conversations with friends, they realised that they'd already been receiving signs, but they hadn't recognised what they were until I'd shared my stories with them. For others, a sign came to them very shortly after we'd had such a conversation and they'd started to open themselves up to the possibility of receiving them. On witnessing one of these signs, someone said to me, 'Once you start recognising the signs, life is never the same again.'

An interviewer once asked me, rather than describing the work I do, to instead explain to him what the significance of it was to me. This is what I now want you to start thinking about with intention: what could the significance of signs be for you? How could they transform the way you live? And how could you bring the elements of this book that have appealed to you into your life?

I've tried to outline the benefits of signs to me and explain the ways in which I think you can access them too – now it's your turn to decide what you want to do with that knowledge. This could be through meditation, journalling, conversations with other people or whatever form of reflection suits you. And this process of reflection will hopefully already have begun for you as you were reading and thinking about the signs in your own life. However, as you progress, you may also wish to dip back into parts of the book to consider some of the suggestions and ideas that you haven't tried yet.

I've gone on a long journey of discovery that has led me to a place where spirituality is more important to me than ever. As we've seen, this began with me going on longer walks in nature and leaning on the support of my inner circle. I also had to reconnect with my intuition, because I'd lost trust in myself, and, over time, I came to realise the importance of beauty in my life and deliberately introduced creative practices into my routine. Along with an effort to tune in to my senses more, these things helped me to better notice the world around me. This has allowed me to get to the point where I am able to see the signs that are sent to me and take full advantage of them, providing me with comfort and guidance and enriching my overall experience of life.

The journey might not be exactly the same for you, and that's okay – you have to discover your own path. Perhaps you find that tapping into your intuition more effectively is enough on its own to improve the way you live your life, or maybe a stronger connection with nature and other people is what gives you the confidence and trust to follow your signs, but creativity and beauty are less important to you. Whatever resonates with you is what I want you to take away from this book, as I believe that this is what will allow you to expand your consciousness and open your mind to the possibility of something greater than us, something you can tap into, and to use the language of signs to trust your instincts, find your purpose and live without limits.

Notes

Preface

1 Love, S., 2 Apr. 2024. Why so many of us see our loved ones after they have died. Psyche. https://psyche.co/ideas/why-so-many-of-us-see-our-loved-ones-after-they-have-died.
2 Hamilton, D. R., 2 Apr. 2015. Can we see dead people? https://drdavidhamilton.com/can-we-see-dead-people/.

Introduction

1 Mind, Jun. 2020. Mental health facts and statistics. https://www.mind.org.uk/information-support/types-of-mental-health-problems/mental-health-facts-and-statistics/.
2 NHS England, 22 Oct. 2020. Mental health of children and young people in England, 2020: Wave 1 follow up to the 2017 survey. https://digital.nhs.uk/data-and-information/publications/statistical/mental-health-of-children-and-young-people-in-england/2020-wave-1-follow-up.
3 Abi-Jaoude, E., Naylor, K. T. and Pignatiello, A., 2020. Smartphones, social media use and youth mental health. *Canadian Medical Association Journal*, 192(6), pp. E136–41.
4 Perlis, R. H., Uslu, A., Schulman, J., Gunning, F. M., Santillana, M., Baum, M. A., Druckman, J. N., Ognyanova, K. and Lazer, D., 2025. Irritability and social media use in US adults. *JAMA Network Open*, 8(1), p. e2452807; Meshi, D., Cotten, S. R. and Bender, A. R., 2020. Problematic social media use and perceived social isolation in older adults: A cross-sectional study. *Gerontology*, 66(2), pp. 160–8.
5 Jung, C., 1960. Synchronicity: An acausal connecting principle. In: *The Structure and Dynamics of the Psyche, Collected Works 8*. Princeton University Press.

Chapter 1

1 Ruini, C. and Mortara, C. C., 2022. Writing technique across psychotherapies – from traditional expressive writing to new positive psychology interventions: A narrative review. *Journal of Contemporary Psychotherapy*, 52(1), pp. 23–34.
2 Long, J., 2014. Near-death experience. Evidence for their reality. *Missouri Medicine*, 111, pp. 372–80.
3 Lim, C. Y., Park, J. Y., Kim, D. Y., Yoo, K. D., Kim, H. J., Kim, Y. and Shin, S. J., 2018. Terminal lucidity in the teaching hospital setting. *Death Studies*, 44(5), pp. 285–91.
4 Batthyány, A., 2024. *Threshold: Terminal Lucidity and the Border between Life and Death*. Scribe Publications.
5 Tucker, J. B., 2021. *Before: Children's Memories of Past Lives*. St Martin's Essentials.
6 Alexander, E., 2012. *Proof of Heaven: A Neurosurgeon's Journey into the Afterlife*. Simon & Schuster.
7 Eagleman, D., 2011. *Incognito: The Secret Lives of the Brain*. Pantheon.
8 Eagleman, D., 2009. *Sum: Forty Tales from the Afterlives*. Canongate Books.
9 Hoffman, D. D., 2010. Sensory experiences as cryptic symbols of a multimodal user interface. *Activitas Nervosa Superior*, 52, pp. 95–104.

Chapter 2

1 Zwicky, A., 7 Aug. 2005. Just between Dr Language and I. Language Log. http://itre.cis.upenn.edu/~myl/languagelog/archives/002386.html.
2 Kershner, K. and Henderson, A., 5 Sep. 2023. What's the Baader-Meinhof phenomenon? HowStuffWorks. https://science.howstuffworks.com/life/inside-the-mind/human-brain/baader-meinhof-phenomenon.htm#pt4.
3 Purcell, A. and Zukerman, Z., 17 Aug. 2011. Brain's synaptic pruning continues into your 20s. New Scientist. https://www.newscientist.com/article/dn20803-brains-synaptic-pruning-continues-into-your-20s/.
4 Gonçalves, J. T., Bloyd, C. W., Shtrahman, M., Johnston, S. T., Schafer, S. T., Parylak, S. L., Tran, T., Chang, T. and Gage, F. H., 2016. *In vivo* imaging of dendritic pruning in dentate granule cells. *Nature Neuroscience*, 19(6), pp. 788–91.
5 Kahneman, D., 2011. *Thinking, Fast and Slow*. Allen Lane.
6 Mithen, S. J., 1990. *Thoughtful Foragers: A Study of Prehistoric Decision Making*. Cambridge University Press.
7 Horr, N. K., Braun, C. and Volz, K. G., 2014. Feeling before knowing why: The role of the orbitofrontal cortex in intuitive judgments – an

MEG study. *Cognitive, Affective, & Behavioral Neuroscience, 14*, pp. 1271–85.
8 Hebb, D. O., 1949. *The Organization of Behavior: A Neuropsychological Theory*. Wiley and Sons.
9 van der Kolk, B., 2014. *The Body Keeps the Score: Mind, Brain and Body in the Transformation of Trauma*. Allen Lane.
10 Dias, B. and Ressler, K., 2014. Parental olfactory experience influences behavior and neural structure in subsequent generations. *Nature Neuroscience, 17*, pp. 89–96.

Chapter 3

1 Ryff, C. D., 1989. Happiness is everything, or is it? Explorations on the meaning of psychological well-being. *Journal of Personality and Social Psychology, 57*(6), pp. 1069–81.
2 Netflix, 2023. *Live to 100: Secrets of the Blue Zones* [documentary].
3 Greyson, B., 2022. *After: A Doctor Explores What Near-Death Experiences Reveal about Life and Beyond*. Penguin.
4 Malůš, M., Kupka, M. and Dostál, D., 2016. Existential meaning in life, mindfulness and self-esteem in the context of restricted environmental stimulation. *Psychology and Its Contexts, 7*(2), pp. 59–72.
5 Ustinova, Y., 2009. Cave experiences and ancient Greek oracles. *Time and Mind, 2*(3), pp. 265–86.
6 Wheal, J., 2021. *Recapture the Rapture: Rethinking God, Sex, and Death in a World That's Lost Its Mind*. Harper.
7 Schacter D. L., 1976. The hypnagogic state: A critical review of the literature. *Psychological Bulletin, 83*(3), pp. 452–81.
8 Laborde, S., Mosley, E. and Thayer, J. F., 2017. Heart rate variability and cardiac vagal tone in psychophysiological research – recommendations for experiment planning, data analysis, and data reporting. *Frontiers in Psychology, 8*, p. 213.
9 Flynn, C., 1986. *After the Beyond*. Prentice Hall.
10 Ring, K., 1995. The impact of near-death experiences on persons who have not had them: A report of a preliminary study and two replications. *Journal of Near-Death Studies, 13*(4), pp. 223–35.
11 Ring, K., 1992. *The Omega Project*. William Morrow; Ring, K., 1995. The impact of near-death experiences on persons who have not had them: A report of a preliminary study and two replications. *Journal of Near-Death Studies, 13*(4), pp. 223–35.
12 Tassell-Matamua, N., Lindsay, N., Bennett, S., Valentine, H. and Pahina, J., 2017. Does learning about near-death experiences promote psycho-spiritual benefits in those who have not had a near-death experience? *Journal of Spirituality in Mental Health, 19*(2), pp. 95–115.

13 World Population Review, 2025. Religious people by country 2025. https://worldpopulationreview.com/country-rankings/religion-by-country.

Chapter 4

1 Adapted from Young, E., 2022. *Super Senses: The Science of Your 32 Senses and How to Use Them.* John Murray.
2 Kawamura, Y. and Kare, M. R., eds., 1987. *Umami: A Basic Taste.* Marcel Dekker Inc.
3 Kipnis, J., 1 Aug. 2018. The seventh sense. Scientific American. https://www.scientificamerican.com/article/the-seventh-sense/.
4 Kokocińska-Kusiak, A., Woszczyło, M., Zybala, M., Maciocha, J., Barłowska, K. and Dzięcioł, M., 2021. Canine olfaction: Physiology, behavior, and possibilities for practical applications. *Animals: An Open Access Journal from MDPI, 11*(8), p. 2463.
5 Wiltschko, W., Munro, U., Ford, H. and Wiltschko, R., 2006. Bird navigation: What type of information does the magnetite-based receptor provide? *Proceedings of the Royal Society B: Biological Sciences, 273*(1603), pp. 2815–20.
6 Stoyanov, G. S., Matev, B. K., Valchanov, P., Sapundzhiev, N. and Young, J. R., 2018. The human vomeronasal (Jacobson's) organ: A short review of current conceptions, with an English translation of Potiquet's original text. *Cureus, 10*(5), p. e2643.
7 Dzięcioł, M., Podgórski, P., Stańczyk, E., Szumny, A., Woszczyło, M., Pieczewska, B., Niżański, W., Nicpoń, J. and Wrzosek, M. A., 2020. MRI features of the vomeronasal organ in dogs (Canis familiaris). *Frontiers in Veterinary Science, 7*, p. 159.
8 Parkinson's UK, 20 Dec. 2017. Meet the woman who can smell Parkinson's. https://www.parkinsons.org.uk/news/meet-woman-who-can-smell-parkinsons.
9 Parkinson's UK, 7 Sep. 2022. 'Smelling Parkinson's' research could make it quicker and easier to diagnose Parkinson's. https://www.parkinsons.org.uk/news/smelling-parkinsons-research-could-make-it-quicker-and-easier-diagnose-parkinsons.
10 Felder-Schmittbuhl, M. P., Buhr, E. D., Dkhissi-Benyahya, O., Hicks, D., Peirson, S. N., Ribelayga, C. P., Sandu, C., Spessert, R. and Tosini, G., 2018. Ocular clocks: Adapting mechanisms for eye functions and health. *Investigative Ophthalmology & Visual Science, 59*(12), pp. 4856–70.
11 UniSci, 27 Feb. 2001. Brain areas critical to human time sense identified. https://www.unisci.com/stories/20011/0227013.htm.
12 Chu, B., Marwaha, K., Sanvictores, T., Awosika, A. O. and Ayers, D., 2024. Physiology, stress reaction. In: *StatPearls [Internet].*

13 Garner, M., Attwood, A., Baldwin, D. S., James, A. and Munafò, M. R., 2011. Inhalation of 7.5% carbon dioxide increases threat processing in humans. *Neuropsychopharmacology*, *36*(8), pp. 1557–62.

14 Gaeta, G. and Wilson, D. A., 2022. Reciprocal relationships between sleep and smell. *Frontiers in Neural Circuits*, *16*, p. 1076354.

15 Woo, C. C., Miranda, B., Sathishkumar, M., Dehkordi-Vakil, F., Yassa, M. A. and Leon, M., 2023. Overnight olfactory enrichment using an odorant diffuser improves memory and modifies the uncinate fasciculus in older adults. *Frontiers in Neuroscience*, *17*, p. 1200448.

16 Kakara, R., Bergen, G., Burns, E. and Stevens, M., 2023. Nonfatal and fatal falls among adults aged ≥65 years – United States, 2020–2021. *Morbidity and Mortality Weekly Report*, *72*, pp. 938–43.

Chapter 5

1 Tozzi, P., 2014. Does fascia hold memories? *Journal of Bodywork and Movement Therapies*, *18*, pp. 259–65.

2 van der Kolk, B., *The Body Keeps the Score*.

3 Ibid.

4 Maté, G., 15 Oct. 2024. *This Past Weekend with Theo Von* [podcast]. https://podcasts.apple.com/gb/podcast/dr-gabor-mat%C3%A9/id1190981360?i=1000673124394.

5 Kozlowska, K., Scher, S. and Helgeland, H., 2020. Treatment interventions I: Working with the body. In: *Functional Somatic Symptoms in Children and Adolescents (Palgrave Texts in Counselling and Psychotherapy)*. Palgrave Macmillan.

6 Mayer, E. A., 2011. Gut feelings: The emerging biology of gut–brain communication. *Nature Reviews Neuroscience*, *12*(8), pp. 453–66.

7 Yatsunenko, T., Rey, F. E., Manary, M. J., Trehan, I., Dominguez-Bello, M. G., Contreras, M., Magris, M., Hidalgo, G., Baldassano, R. N., Anokhin, A. P. and Heath, A. C., 2012. Human gut microbiome viewed across age and geography. *Nature*, *486*(7402), pp. 222–7.

8 Bogaert, D., Van Beveren, G. J., de Koff, E. M., Parga, P. L., Lopez, C. E. B., Koppensteiner, L., Clerc, M., Hasrat, R., Arp, K., Chu, M. L. J. and de Groot, P. C., 2023. Mother-to-infant microbiota transmission and infant microbiota development across multiple body sites. *Cell Host & Microbe*, *31*(3), pp. 447–60.

9 Chong, H. Y., Tan, L. T. H., Law, J. W. F., Hong, K. W., Ratnasingam, V., Ab Mutalib, N. S., Lee, L. H. and Letchumanan, V., 2022. Exploring the potential of human milk and formula milk on infants' gut and health. *Nutrients*, *14*(17), p. 3554.

10 Appleton, J., 2018. The gut–brain axis: Influence of microbiota on mood and mental health. *Integrative Medicine (Encinitas, Calif.)*, 17(4), pp. 28–32.

11 Wiertsema, S. P., van Bergenhenegouwen, J., Garssen, J. and Knippels, L. M. J., 2021. The interplay between the gut microbiome and the immune system in the context of infectious diseases throughout life and the role of nutrition in optimizing treatment strategies. *Nutrients*, 13(3), p. 886.

12 De Luca, F. and Shoenfeld, Y., 2019. The microbiome in autoimmune diseases. *Clinical and Experimental Immunology*, 195(1), pp. 74–85.

13 Agirman, G., Yu, K. B. and Hsiao, E. Y., 2021. Signaling inflammation across the gut–brain axis. *Science*, 374(6571), pp. 1087–92.

14 Oligschlaeger, Y., Yadati, T., Houben, T., Condello Oliván, C. M. and Shiri-Sverdlov, R., 2019. Inflammatory bowel disease: A stressed 'gut/feeling'. *Cells*, 8(7), p. 659.

15 Matisz, C. E. and Gruber, A. J., 2022. Neuroinflammatory remodeling of the anterior cingulate cortex as a key driver of mood disorders in gastrointestinal disease and disorders. *Neuroscience and Biobehavioral Reviews*, 133, p. 104497.

16 Luissint, A. C., Parkos, C. A. and Nusrat, A., 2016. Inflammation and the intestinal barrier: Leukocyte-epithelial cell interactions, cell junction remodeling, and mucosal repair. *Gastroenterology*, 151(4), pp. 616–32.

17 Swart, T., 17 Sep. 2019. What you need to know about your brain and probiotics. Forbes. https://www.forbes.com/sites/taraswart/2019/09/17/what-you-need-to-know-about-your-brain-and-probiotics/.

18 Newman, T., 24 Apr. 2024. Does exercise change your gut microbiome? ZOE. https://zoe.com/learn/exercise-gut-microbiome.

19 National Sleep Foundation, 1 Oct. 2020. How much sleep do you really need? https://www.thensf.org/how-many-hours-of-sleep-do-you-really-need/.

20 Jacobs, J. P., Gupta, A., Bhatt, R. R., Brawer, J., Gao, K., Tillisch, K., Lagishetty, V., Firth, R., Gudleski, G. D., Ellingson, B. M. and Labus, J. S., 2021. Cognitive behavioral therapy for irritable bowel syndrome induces bidirectional alterations in the brain-gut-microbiome axis associated with gastrointestinal symptom improvement. *Microbiome*, 9, p. 236.

21 Cleveland Clinic, 2 Oct. 2022. Adaptogens. https://my.clevelandclinic.org/health/drugs/22361-adaptogens.

22 Bell, L., Whyte, A., Duysburgh, C., Marzorati, M., Van den Abbeele, P., Le Cozannet, R., Fança-Berthon, P., Fromentin, E. and Williams, C., 2022. A randomized, placebo-controlled trial investigating the acute and chronic benefits of American Ginseng (Cereboost®) on mood and cognition in healthy young adults, including in vitro

investigation of gut microbiota changes as a possible mechanism of action. *European Journal of Nutrition*, *61*(1), pp. 413–28.

23 Shi, M., Ma, J., Jin, S., Wang, T., Sui, Y. and Chen, L., 2024. Effects of saponins Rb$_1$ and Re in *American ginseng* combined intervention on immune system of aging model. *Frontiers in Molecular Biosciences*, *11*, p. 1392868.

24 Arring, N. M., Millstine, D., Marks, L. A. and Nail, L. M., 2018. Ginseng as a treatment for fatigue: A systematic review. *Journal of Alternative and Complementary Medicine*, *24*(7), pp. 624–33.

25 Amsterdam, J. D. and Panossian, A. G., 2016. Rhodiola rosea L. as a putative botanical antidepressant. *Phytomedicine: International Journal of Phytotherapy and Phytopharmacology*, *23*(7), pp. 770–83.

26 Seweryn, E., Ziała, A. and Gamian, A., 2021. Health-promoting of polysaccharides extracted from *Ganoderma lucidum*. *Nutrients*, *13*(8), p. 2725.

27 Xiuhong, Z., Yue, Z., Shuyan, Y. and Zhonghua, Z., 2015. Effect of Inonotus Obliquus Polysaccharides on physical fatigue in mice. *Journal of Traditional Chinese Medicine*, *35*(4), pp. 468–72.

28 Panossian, A. G., Efferth, T., Shikov, A. N., Pozharitskaya, O. N., Kuchta, K., Mukherjee, P. K., Banerjee, S., Heinrich, M., Wu, W., Guo, D. A. and Wagner, H., 2021. Evolution of the adaptogenic concept from traditional use to medical systems: Pharmacology of stress- and aging-related diseases. *Medicinal Research Reviews*, *41*(1), pp. 630–703.

29 Salve, J., Pate, S., Debnath, K. and Langade, D., 2019. Adaptogenic and anxiolytic effects of ashwagandha root extract in healthy adults: A double-blind, randomized, placebo-controlled clinical study. *Cureus* *11*(12), p. e6466.

30 Ramakrishnan, S., 2024. *The Neuroscience of Tarot: From Imagery to Intuition to Prediction*. Llewellyn Publications.

Chapter 6

1 Sarasso, P., Francesetti, G. and Schoeller, F., 2023. Possible applications of neuroaesthetics to normal and pathological behaviour. *Frontiers in Neuroscience*, *17*, p. 1225308.

2 Lewis, J., 2015. A cross-cultural perspective on the significance of music and dance to culture and society: Insight from BaYaka Pygmies. In: Arbib, M. A., ed. *Language, Music, and the Brain: A Mysterious Relationship*. MIT Press Scholarship Online.

3 Lewis-Williams, J. D., Bardill, P. N., Biesele, M., Yearwood, S., Clegg, J., Davis, W., Groenfeldt, D., Inskeep, R. R., Jones, T., Pretty, G. and Sauvet, G., 1982. The economic and social context of Southern San rock art [and comments and reply]. *Current Anthropology*, *23*(4), pp. 429–49.

4 Fuentes, A., 2017. *The Creative Spark: How Imagination Made Humans Exceptional*. Penguin.

5 Worrall, S., 23 Apr. 2017. How creativity drives human evolution. National Geographic. https://www.nationalgeographic.com/culture/article/creative-spark-augustin-fuentes-evolution.

6 Kaimal, G., Ray, K. and Muniz, J., 2016. Reduction of cortisol levels and participants' responses following art making. *Art Therapy: Journal of the American Art Therapy Association*, 33(2), pp. 74–80; Stuckey, H. L. and Nobel, J., 2010. The connection between art, healing, and public health: A review of current literature. *American Journal of Public Health*, 100(2), pp. 254–63.

7 Orlandi, A. and Candidi, M., 2023. Towards a neuroaesthetics of interactions: A perspective review. https://osf.io/preprints/psyarxiv/fr6mt_v1.

8 Fancourt, D. and Steptoe, A., 2019. The art of life and death: 14 year follow-up analyses of associations between arts engagement and mortality in the English Longitudinal Study of Ageing. *BMJ*, 367, p. l6377.

9 Miller, K. D., 18 Jun. 2019. 14 benefits of practicing gratitude (incl. journaling). PositivePsychology.com. https://positivepsychology.com/benefits-of-gratitude/.

10 Chavda, V. P., Feehan, J. and Apostolopoulos, V., 2024. Inflammation: The cause of all diseases. *Cells*, 13(22), p. 1906.

11 Magsamen, S. and Ross, I., 2023. *Your Brain on Art: How the Arts Transform Us*. Canongate, p. 15.

12 Kim, S. C. and Choi, M. J., 2023. Does the sound of a singing bowl synchronize meditational brainwaves in the listeners? *International Journal of Environmental Research and Public Health*, 20(12), p. 6180; Abhang, P. A., Gawali, B. W. and Mehrotra, S. C., 2016. *Introduction to EEG- and Speech-Based Emotion Recognition*. Academic Press.

13 Trivedi, G., Sharma, K., Saboo, B., Kathirvel, S., Konat, A., Zapadia, V., Prajapati, P. J., Benani, U., Patel, K. and Shah, S., 2023. Humming (simple Bhramari Pranayama) as a stress buster: A holter-based study to analyze heart rate variability (HRV) parameters during Bhramari, physical activity, emotional stress, and sleep. *Cureus*, 15(4), p. e37527.

14 Marie, D., Müller, C. A., Altenmüller, E., Van De Ville, D., Jünemann, K., Scholz, D. S., Krüger, T. H., Worschech, F., Kliegel, M., Sinke, C. and James, C. E., 2023. Music interventions in 132 healthy older adults enhance cerebellar grey matter and auditory working memory, despite general brain atrophy. *Neuroimage: Reports*, 3(2), p. 100166.

15 Schlaug, G., Jäncke, L., Huang, Y., Staiger, J. F. and Steinmetz, H., 1995. Increased corpus callosum size in musicians. *Neuropsychologia*, *33*(8), pp. 1047–55.

16 Noetel, M., Sanders, T., Gallardo-Gómez, D., Taylor, P., del Pozo Cruz, B., Van Den Hoek, D., Smith, J. J., Mahoney, J., Spathis, J., Moresi, M. and Pagano, R., 2024. Effect of exercise for depression: Systematic review and network meta-analysis of randomised controlled trials. *BMJ*, *384*, p. e075847.

17 van der Kolk, B., *The Body Keeps the Score*.

18 Abbing, A., Ponstein, A., van Hooren, S., de Sonneville, L., Swaab, H. and Baars, E., 2018. The effectiveness of art therapy for anxiety in adults: A systematic review of randomised and non-randomised controlled trials. *PloS One*, *13*(12), p. e0208716.

19 Coholic, D., Schinke, R., Oghene, O., Dano, K., Jago, M., McAlister, H. and Grynspan, P., 2019. Arts-based interventions for youth with mental health challenges. *Journal of Social Work*, *20*(3), pp. 269–86.

20 Berns, G. S., Blaine, K., Prietula, M. J. and Pye, B. E., 2013. Short- and long-term effects of a novel on connectivity in the brain. *Brain Connectivity*, *3*(6), pp. 590–600.

21 Djikic, M., Oatley, K. and Moldoveanu, M. C., 2013. Reading other minds: Effects of literature on empathy. *Scientific Study of Literature*, *3*(1), pp. 28–47.

22 Carney, J. and Robertson, C., 2022. Five studies evaluating the impact on mental health and mood of recalling, reading, and discussing fiction. *PloS One*, *17*(4), p. e0266323.

Chapter 7

1 Magsamen, S. and Ross, I., *Your Brain on Art: How the Arts Transform Us*, p. 15.

2 Diamond, M. C., Krech, D. and Rosenzweig, M. R., 1964. The effects of an enriched environment on the histology of the rat cerebral cortex. *Journal of Comparative Neurology*, *123*(1), pp. 111–20.

3 Magsamen, S. and Ross, I., *Your Brain on Art: How the Arts Transform Us*, p. 15.

4 Evitts Dickinson, E., 2019. Beauty and the brain. Johns Hopkins Magazine. https://hub.jhu.edu/magazine/2019/fall/neuroaesthetics-suchi-reddy-ivy-ross-susan-magsamen/.

5 Ikei, H., Song, C. and Miyazaki, Y., 2017. Physiological effects of touching wood. *International Journal of Environmental Research and Public Health*, *14*(7), p. 801.

6 Vartanian, O., Navarrete, G., Chatterjee, A., Fich, L. B., Gonzalez-Mora, J. L., Leder, H., Modroño, C., Nadal, M., Rostrup, N. and Skov,

M., 2015. Architectural design and the brain: Effects of ceiling height and perceived enclosure on beauty judgments and approach-avoidance decisions. *Journal of Environmental Psychology*, 41, pp. 10–18.

7 Bar, M. and Neta, M., 2006. Humans prefer curved visual objects. *Psychological Science*, 17(8), pp. 645–8.

8 Hunter, M. R., Gillespie, B. W. and Chen, S. Y. P., 2019. Urban nature experiences reduce stress in the context of daily life based on salivary biomarkers. *Frontiers in Psychology*, 10, p. 413490.

9 Carrington, D., 4 Sep. 2024. 'Better than medication': Prescribing nature works, project shows. Guardian. https://www.theguardian.com/environment/article/2024/sep/04/better-than-medication-prescribing-nature-works-project-shows.

10 Bratman, G. N., Hamilton, J. P., Hahn, K. S., Daily, G. C. and Gross, J. J., 2015. Nature experience reduces rumination and subgenual prefrontal cortex activation. *Proceedings of the National Academy of Sciences of the United States of America*, 112(28), pp. 8567–72.

11 Song, C., Ikei, H. and Miyazaki, Y., 2016. Physiological effects of nature therapy: A review of the research in Japan. *International Journal of Environmental Research and Public Health*, 13(8), p. 781.

12 Igarashi, M., Aga, M., Ikei, H., Namekawa, T. and Miyazaki, T., 2015. Physiological and psychological effects on high school students of viewing real and artificial pansies. *International Journal of Environmental Research and Public Health*, 12(3), pp. 2521–31.

13 Chevalier, G., Sinatra, S. T., Oschman, J. L., Sokal, K. and Sokal, P., 2012. Earthing: Health implications of reconnecting the human body to the Earth' s surface electrons. *Journal of Environmental and Public Health*, 2012(1), p. 291541.

14 Koniver, L., 2023. Practical applications of grounding to support health. *Biomedical Journal*, 46(1), pp. 41–7.

15 Winterman, D., 8 May 2013. The surprising uses for birdsong. BBC News. https://www.bbc.co.uk/news/magazine-22298779.

16 Lynn, C., 2014. Hearth and campfire influences on arterial blood pressure: Defraying the costs of the social brain through fireside relaxation. *Evolutionary Psychology*, 12(5), pp. 983–1003.

17 Walski, T., Dąbrowska, K., Drohomirecka, A., Jędruchniewicz, N., Trochanowska-Pauk, N., Witkiewicz, W. and Komorowska, M., 2019. The effect of red-to-near-infrared (R/NIR) irradiation on inflammatory processes. *International Journal of Radiation Biology*, 95(9), pp. 1326–36.

18 Allansdottir, H., 17 Apr. 2024. Star-gazing: How astronomy can change your life. TheArticle. https://www.thearticle.com/star-gazing-how-astronomy-can-change-your-life.

19 Lowry, C. A., Hollis, J. H., De Vries, A., Pan, B., Brunet, L. R., Hunt, J. R., Paton, J. F., van Kampen, E., Knight, D. M., Evans, A. K.

and Rook, G. A., 2007. Identification of an immune-responsive mesolimbocortical serotonergic system: Potential role in regulation of emotional behavior. *Neuroscience*, *146*(2), pp. 756–72.

20 Garden Health, 2025. Top 10 air purifying houseplants. https://www. gardenhealth.com/advice/houseplant-care/top-ten-air-purifying-houseplants.

21 Mostajeran, F., Krzikawski, J., Steinicke, F. and Kühn, S., 2021. Effects of exposure to immersive videos and photo slideshows of forest and urban environments. *Scientific Reports*, *11*(1), p. 3994.

22 Holewinski, B., n.d. Underground networking: The amazing connections beneath your feet [blog]. National Forest Foundation. https://www.nationalforests.org/blog/underground-mycorrhizal-network.

23 Wai, Y. C. and Chao, E. C., 2023. Bioacoustics as forms of resistance: Growing mycelium instruments and mushroom communication in a high-tech city-state. *East Asian Science, Technology and Society: An International Journal*, *17*(1), pp. 105–10; Genç, Ç., Launne, E. and Häkkilä, J., Oct. 2022. Interactive mycelium composites: Material exploration on combining mushroom with off-the-shelf electronic components. In: Nordic Human-Computer Interaction Conference (NordiCHI '22). *Association for Computing Machinery*, *19*, pp. 1–12.

24 Mithöfer, A. and Boland, W., 2012. Plant defense against herbivores: Chemical aspects. *Annual Review of Plant Biology*, *63*(1), pp. 431–50.

25 Tsao, T. M., Tsai, M. J., Hwang, J. S., Cheng, W. F., Wu, C. F., Chou, C. K. and Su, T. C., 2018. Health effects of a forest environment on natural killer cells in humans: An observational pilot study. *Oncotarget*, *9*(23), pp. 16501–11.

26 Li, Q., Kobayashi, M., Wakayama, Y., Inagaki, H., Katsumata, M., Hirata, Y., Hirata, K., Shimizu, T., Kawada, T., Park, B. J., Ohira, T., Kagawa, T. and Miyazaki, Y., 2009. Effect of phytoncide from trees on human natural killer cell function. *International Journal of Immunopathology and Pharmacology*, *22*(4), pp. 951–9.

27 Bhaumik, S., 20 Jan. 2005. Tsunami folklore 'saved islanders'. BBC News. http://news.bbc.co.uk/1/hi/world/south_asia/4181855.stm.

28 McKie, R., 30 Nov. 2024. Can goats predict earthquakes? Can dogs forecast volcanic eruptions? These scientists think so. Guardian. https://www.theguardian.com/science/2024/nov/30/can-goats-predict-earthquakes-can-dogs-forecast-volcanic-eruptions-these-scientists-think-so.

29 Luppi, A. I., Girn, M., Rosas, F. E., Timmermann, C., Roseman, L., Erritzoe, D., Nutt, D. J., Stamatakis, E. A., Spreng, R. N., Xing, L. and Huttner, W. B., 2024. A role for the serotonin 2A receptor in the expansion and functioning of human transmodal cortex. *Brain*, *147*(1), pp. 56–80.

30 Carhart-Harris, R. L., Muthukumaraswamy, S., Roseman, L., Kaelen, M., Droog, W., Murphy, K., Tagliazucchi, E., Schenberg, E. E., Nest, T., Orban, C. and Leech, R., 2016. Neural correlates of the LSD experience revealed by multimodal neuroimaging. *Proceedings of the National Academy of Sciences*, 113(17), pp. 4853–8.

31 Petri, G., Expert, P., Turkheimer, F., Carhart-Harris, R., Nutt, D., Hellyer, P. J. and Vaccarino, F., 2014. Homological scaffolds of brain functional networks. *Journal of the Royal Society, Interface*, 11(101), p. 20140873.

32 Bahi, C., Irrmischer, M., Franken, K., Fejer, G., Schlenker, A., Deijen, J. B. and Engelbregt, H., 2024. Effects of conscious connected breathing on cortical brain activity, mood and state of consciousness in healthy adults. *Current Psychology*, 43(12), pp. 10578–89.

Chapter 8

1 Ghaderi, A., Tabatabaei, S. M., Nedjat, S., Javadi, M. and Larijani, B., 2018. Explanatory definition of the concept of spiritual health: A qualitative study in Iran. *Journal of Medical Ethics and History of Medicine*, 11, p. 3.

2 Samson, D. R., 2021. The human sleep paradox: The unexpected sleeping habits of Homo sapiens. *Annual Review of Anthropology*, 50(1), pp. 259–74.

3 Malinsky-Buller, A. and Hovers, E., 2019. One size does not fit all: Group size and the late middle Pleistocene prehistoric archive. *Journal of Human Evolution*, 127, pp. 118–32.

4 Gallup, Inc., 2023. The global state of social connections. https://www.gallup.com/analytics/509675/state-of-social-connections.aspx.

5 Wang, F., Gao, Y., Han, Z., Yu, Y., Long, Z., Jiang, X., Wu, Y., Pei, B., Cao, Y., Ye, J. and Wang, M., 2023. A systematic review and meta-analysis of 90 cohort studies of social isolation, loneliness and mortality. *Nature Human Behaviour*, 7(8), pp. 1307–19.

6 Offord, C., 13 Jul. 2020. How social isolation affects the brain. The University of Chicago. https://psychiatry.uchicago.edu/news/how-social-isolation-affects-brain.

7 Erkens, V. A., Nater, U. M., Hennig, J. and Häusser, J. A., 2019. Social identification and contagious stress reactions. *Psychoneuroendocrinology*, 102, pp. 58–62.

8 Wedekind, C., Seebeck, T., Bettens, F. and Paepke, A. J., 1995. MHC-dependent mate preferences in humans. *Proceedings of the Royal Society of London. Series B: Biological Sciences*, 260(1359), pp. 245–9.

9 Gobrogge, K. and Wang, Z., 2016. The ties that bond: Neurochemistry of attachment in voles. *Current Opinion in Neurobiology*, 38, pp. 80–8.

10 Coghlan, A., 16 Jun. 2008. Gay brains structured like those of the opposite sex. New Scientist. https://www.newscientist.com/article/dn14146-gay-brains-structured-like-those-of-the-opposite-sex.

11 Dunbar, R., 2021. *Friends: Understanding the Power of Our Most Important Relationships*. Little, Brown.

12 Honigsbaum, M., 21 Aug. 2011. Oxytocin: Could the 'trust hormone' rebond our troubled world? Guardian. https://www.theguardian.com/science/2011/aug/21/oxytocin-zak-neuroscience-trust-hormone.

13 Liu, S., Smit, D. J., Abdellaoui, A., van Wingen, G. A. and Verweij, K. J., 2023. Brain structure and function show distinct relations with genetic predispositions to mental health and cognition. *Biological Psychiatry: Cognitive Neuroscience and Neuroimaging*, 8(3), pp. 300–10.

Acknowledgements

To all my friends and family, and Robin's friends who have supported me since his illness and passing. There are too many of you to mention, but you know who you are. Thank you and I love you.

Thank you to Paul Murphy for helping me tell my story.

Thank you to Joel Rickett, Leah Feltham, Julia Kellaway and the team at Penguin Random House UK.

Thank you to Steven Bartlett, Rik Ubhi, Georgie Holt, Christiana Brenton and the team at Flight Books.

Thank you to Judith Curr for believing in me and Nina Shield, Julia Kent and the team at HarperOne USA.

Thank you for specific bits of advice and support to: Dr Fritz Swart, Nicola Tyler, Dr Etienne van der Walt, Saskia Wheeler, Simon Salter, Alice Law, Jamie Clements, Sabrina Percy, Tracie Bryant, Deodata Semionovate, Dr Rupy Aujla, Emilie Cochrane, Rosie Underwood, Idris Blac, Dr Jenna Macciochi, Dr Grazyna Soderbom, Matthew Ball and Dr Ayan Panja.

Thank you to Idris Blac for creating the music to help me write this book.

Index

217